DΣ ANIMA
(Of the Soul)

Translated
and with commentary
by
Robert Drew Hicks
Cambridge University

ARISTOTLE

British Library Cataloguing in Publication Data
A catalogue record for this book is available from the British Library

ISBN-13: 978-1-909735-95-8

Printed and bound in Great Britain by Lightning Source UK Ltd., 6 Precedent Drive, Rooksley, Milton Keynes MK13 8PR.

Illustrations

Front cover: *The School of Athens*, fresco by Raphael (Raffaello Sanzio), 1511, in the Stanza della Segratura, Vatican Palace, Rome

Back cover: *Aristotle*, Raphael

Title page: *Knowledge of Causes,* fresco by Raphael, 1511, the ceiling of the Stanza della Segnatura above *The School of Athens*, Vatican Palace, Rome

Book I image: Hermes Psychostasia (Weigher of Souls) stands between Memnon and Achilles (not shown) in the Trojan War, weighing their respective destinies on the scales of fate. Greek vase, arehaic

Book II image: Charon, dead souls' guide to the underworld. Greek vase, 4th. century B.C.

Book III image: *The Poet* or *The Thinker, (The Gates of Hell)*, Auguste Rodin, 1880-c.1890

CONTENTS

Short Biography of Aristotle	5
Commentary on *De Anima* by R.D. Hicks	8

De Anima

Book I

Chapter 1	52
Chapter 2	55
Chapter 3	58
Chapter 4	62
Chapter 5	65

Book II

Chapter 1	72
Chapter 2	74
Chapter 3	76
Chapter 4	77
Chapter 5	80
Chapter 6	82
Chapter 7	83
Chapter 8	85
Chapter 9	88
Chapter 10	89
Chapter 11	90
Chapter 12	93

Book III

Chapter 1	96
Chapter 2	98
Chapter 3	100
Chapter 4	103
Chapter 5	105
Chapter 6	106
Chapter 7	107
Chapter 8	108
Chapter 9	109
Chapter 10	111
Chapter 11	112
Chapter 12	113
Chapter 13	115

SHORT BIOGRAPHY OF ARISTOTLE
(Greek: Ἀριστοτέλης, Aristotélēs)
(384 BC – 322 BC)

About the time that Hippocrates died, Aristotle, who may be regarded as the founder of the science of "Natural History", was born (B.C. 384) in Stagira, an unimportant Hellenic colony in Thrace, near the Macedonian frontier. His father was a distinguished physician, and, like Hippocrates, boasted descent from the Asclepiadæ. The importance attached by the Asclepiads to the habit of physical observation, which has been already referred to in the life of Hippocrates, secured for Aristotle, from his earliest years, that familiarity with biological studies which is so clearly evident in many of his works.

Both parents of Aristotle died when their son was still a youth, and in consequence of this he went to reside with Proxenus, a native of Atarneus, who had settled at Stagira. Subsequently he went to Athens and joined the school of Plato. Here he remained for about twenty years, and applied himself to study with such energy that he became pre-eminent even in that distinguished band of philosophers. He is said to have been spoken of by Plato as "the intellect" of the school, and to have been compared by him to a spirited colt that required the application of the rein to restrain its ardour.

Aristotle probably wrote at this time some philosophical works, the fame of which reached the ears of Philip, King of Macedonia, and added to the reputation which the young philosopher had already made with that monareh; for Philip is said to have written to him on the occasion of Alexander's birth, B.C. 356:

"King Philip of Macedonia to Aristotle, greeting. Know that a son has been born to me. I thank the gods not so much that they have given him to me, as that they have permitted him to be born in the time of Aristotle. I hope that thou wilt form him to be a king worthy to succeed me and to rule the Macedonians."

After the death of Plato, which occurred in 347 B.C., Aristotle quitted Athens and went to Atarneus, where he stayed with Hermias, who was then despot of that town. Hermias was a remarkable man, who, from being a slave, had contrived to raise himself to the supreme power. He had been at Athens and had heard Plato's lectures, and had there formed a friendship for Aristotle. With this man the philosopher remained for three years, and was then compelled suddenly to seek refuge in Mitylene, owing to the perfidious murder of Hermias. The latter was decoyed out of the town by the Persian general, seized and sent prisoner to Artaxerxes, by whom he was hanged as a rebel. On leaving Atarneus, Aristotle took with him a niece of Hermias, named Pythias, whom he afterwards married. She died young, leaving an infant daughter.

Two or three years after this, Aristotle became tutor to Alexander, who was then about thirteen years old. The philosopher seems to have been a favourite with both the king and the prince, and, in gratitude for his services, Philip rebuilt Stagira and restored it to its former inhabitants, who had either been dispersed or carried into slavery. The king is said also to have established there a school for Aristotle. The high respect in which Alexander held his teacher is expressed in his saying that he honoured him no less than his own father, for while to one he owed life, to the other he owed all that made life valuable.

In 336 B.C. Alexander, who was then only about twenty years of age, became king, and Aristotle soon afterwards quitted Macedonia and took up his residence in Athens once more, after an absence of about twelve years. Here he opened a school in the Lycæum, a gymnasium on the eastern side of the city, and continued his work there for about twelve years, during which time Alexander was making his brilliant conquests. The lectures were given for the most part while walking in the garden, and in consequence, perhaps, of this, the sect received the name of the Peripatetics. The discourses were of two kinds - the esoteric, or abstruse, and the exoteric, or familiar; the former being delivered to the more advanced pupils only. During the greater part of this time Aristotle kept up correspondence with Alexander, who is said to have placed at his disposal thousands of men, who were busily employed in collecting objects and in making observations for the completion of the philosopher's zoological researches. Alexander is, moreover, said to have given the philosopher eight hundred talents for the same purpose.

In spite of these marks of friendship and respect, Alexander, who was fast becoming intoxicated with success, and corrupted by Asiatic influences, gradually cooled in his attachment towards Aristotle. This may have been hastened by several causes, and among others by the freedom of speech and republican opinions of Callisthenes, a kinsman and disciple of Aristotle, who had been, by the latter's influence, appointed to attend on Alexander. Callisthenes proved so unpopular, that the king seems to have availed himself readily of the first plausible pretext for putting him to death, and to have threatened his former friend and teacher with a similar punishment. The latter, for his part, probably had a deep feeling of resentment towards the destroyer of his kinsman.

Meanwhile the Athenians knew nothing of these altered relations between Aristotle and Alexander, but continued to regard the philosopher as thoroughly imbued with kingly notions (in spite of his writings being quite to the contrary); so that he was an object of suspicion and dislike to the Athenian patriots. Nevertheless, as long as Alexander was alive, Aristotle was safe from molestation. As soon, however, as Alexander's death became known, the anti-Macedonian feeling of the Athenians burst forth, and found a victim in the philosopher. A charge of impiety was brought against him. It was alleged that he had paid divine honours to his wife Pythias and to his friend Hermias. Now, for the latter, a eunuch, who from the rank of a slave had raised himself to the position of despot over a free Grecian community, so far from coupling his name (as Aristotle had done in his hymn) with the greatest personages of Hellenic mythology, the Athenian public felt that no contempt was too bitter. To escape the storm the philosopher retired to Chalcis, in Eubœa, then under garrison by Antipater, the Governor of Macedonia, remarking in a letter, written afterwards, that he did so in order that the Athenians might not have the opportunity of sinning a second time against philosophy (the allusion being, of course, to the fate of Socrates).

He probably intended to return to Athens again as soon as the political troubles had abated, but in September, 322 B.C., he died at Chalcis. An overwrought mind, coupled with indigestion and weakness of the stomach, from which he had long suffered, was most probably the cause of death. Some of his detractors, however, have asserted that he took poison, and others that he drowned himself in the Eubœan Euripus.

It is not easy to arrive at a just estimate of the character of Aristotle. By some of his successors he has been reproached with ingratitude to his teacher, Plato; with servility to Macedonian power, and with love of costly display. How far these two last charges are due to personal slander it is impossible to say. The only ground for the first charge is, that he criticised adversely some of Plato's doctrines.

The manuscripts of Aristotle's works passed through many vicissitudes. At the death of the philosopher they were bequeathed to Theophrastus, who continued chief of the Peripatetic school for thirty-five years. Theophrastus left them, with his own works, to a philosophical friend and pupil, Neleus, who conveyed them from Athens to his residence at Scepsis, in Asia Minor. About thirty or forty years after the death of Theophrastus, the kings of Pergamus, to whom the city of Scepsis belonged, began collecting books to form a library on the Alexandrian plan. This led the heirs of Neleus to conceal their literary treasures in a cellar, and there the manuscripts remained for nearly a century and a half, exposed to injury from damp and worms. At length they were sold to Apellicon, a resident at Athens, who was attached to the Peripatetic sect. Many of the manuscripts were imperfect, having become worm-eaten or illegible. These defects Apellicon attempted to remedy; but, being a lover of books rather than a philosopher, he performed the work somewhat unskilfully. When Athens was taken by Sylla in 86 B.C., the library of Apellicon was transported to Rome. There various literary Greeks obtained access to it; and, among others, Tyrannion, a grammarian and friend of Cicero, did good service in the work of correction. Andronicus of Rhodes afterwards arranged the whole into sections, and published the manuscripts with a tabulated list.

Charles McRae
Excerpt from: Fathers of Biology, 1890

COMMENTARY
On the subject matter of *De Anima*

This treatise, however inadequate its method and assumptions, when judged by the standard of the present day, has nevertheless a recognised place in the early history of psychology, for it is the outcome of a long series of conjectures, enquiries and provisional hypotheses, which occupied men's minds in the infancy of science. Aristitle himself, though he may be claimed as in some sort the founder of a science of psychology, comes at the end of a period of development and, to understand him aright, we must not only take account of the thinkers who preceded him, but also seek the humble origins of their speculations in the crude conceptions of the distant past. Anthropology has made us familiar with the fundemental conception of the soul as a duplicate of the man or thing to whom it belongs. So far as it is possible to retrace the steps by which this conclusion is reached, it would seem that savages assimilate inanimate to animate objects. In natural phenomena the savage sees the agency of personal beings, whom he believes to be swayed by the same motives and impulses as himself. This applies to all vital and mental phenomena. Activity in animals and other men is explained by the presence within them, sleep and death by the absence from them, of something which the observer conceives as, like himself, a concrete material thing, a miniature of the body, seen in dreams, in shadows, in reflections, liable to come and go from the body in which it resides, and finally severed from it at death. That it survived the body was a widespread belief, attested by the cults of many races, by the practice of burying with the dead, articles for use and comfort to which they had been accustomed in their lives, and by the kindred practice of human and animal sacrifices at the funeral rites of chiefs. It is quite certain that the Greeks were no exception to the universality of these beliefs. In the legends of Meleager and Nisus the external soul, on which the life of the individual depends, plays the same part as in the folk-lore of savages today. The opening lines of the *Iliad* draw a sharp distinction between the heroes themselves, left a prey for dogs and vultures, and their souls, sent down to Hades or the invisible world. The ghost of Patroclus, which appears to Achilles in a dream, is an emaciated, enfeebled shadow, deprived of all its strength by severance from the body, which was the real man. In the underworld these pale, ineffectual ghosts are much alike in general condition. Apart from a few notorious offenders punished for their misdeeds, they pursue the shadows of their former avocations. Whether in Greek language and thought two separate conceptions are blended, whether the sum of the intellectual and moral qualities was associated at one time with the blood and at another with the breath, whether the breath of life superseded an older smoke-soul, the exhalation arising from spilt blood, and whether these two conceptions were connected with the practices of inhumation and cremation respectively, are matters of speculation on which it is hardly possible to arrive at a definite conclusion. When we pass from Homer to later poets we find the same primitive beliefs variously modified. In Hesiod the heroes go no longer to the underworld, but to the Isles of the Blest, and ancestral spirits have developed into "daemons" exerting a beneficent influence on their descendants. From the dirges of Pindar we have two important fragments. One is a glowing picture of the lot of the happy dead. In the other we are told that, "while the body of every man followeth after mighty death, there still liveth a likeness of his prime which alone is of divine origin, which slumbereth so long as the limbs are busy, but full oft in dreams showeth to sleepers the issue that draweth near of pleasant things and cruel".

In the Orphic and Pythagorean brotherhoods the primitive beliefs were moulded into a thoroughgoing doctrine of transmigration. Three main conceptions underlie Orphic asceticism. First, there is the opposition between body and soul. The soul is better than the body and is buried in the body for its sins, the body is its temporary prison. Next comes the necessity for a purification of the soul. All evil is followed by retribution. Through abstinence and penance alone may the soul hope to regain its former blissful state. Thirdly, there is the long series of incarnations in which, according to their deeds during a former existence, souls take a higher or a lower place in human or animal bodies or even in plants. Though these ideas occupy so small a place in literature, they are clearly very old, for the extant burlesque of Xenophanes attests the acceptance of metempsychosis by Pythagoras, and all probability points to his having derived it from the still older Orphic sect. At Athens the Eleusinian mysteries, at which some such ideas were symbolically inculcated, were under the patronage of the state; but nevertheless the belief in an after life in the underworld, as set forth by Homer, for the most part maintained its hold upon the ordinary educated citizen.

Little is to be learned from the Ionian thinkers, whom Ionian Aristotle calls physicists or physiologists. In the dawn of enquiries which, strictly speaking, were rather scientific than philosophical, men sought to explain to themselves of what things were constituted and how they had come into their present condition. Their problem, we should now say, was the constitution of matter and, if occasionally, when they found the primary element in air or fire or some other body, they also declared that this was the cause of vital functions, it was merely a corollary to their general doctrine and of no special importance. The subjects on which we find hints are the substance of the soul, the distinction between its various powers, and the nature of knowledge. So far as the substance of the individual soul was identical with, or a product of, the universal element, they all agreed in regarding it as not immaterial, but of an extremely refined and mobile materiality. The soul was credited with the power to know and perceive, as well as the power to move the body. Heraclitus, who had grasped the flux of matter in constant circulation, held it to be governed by an universal law. Knowledge to him consists in apprehending this law. In comparison with such knowledge he deprecated the evidence of sense: eyes and ears are better than the other senses, but are bad witnesses, if the soul does not understand. Meanwhile in the West other schools of philosophy had arisen, the Eleatic and Pythagorean. Xenophanes distinguished between truth and opinion. Parmenides derived the intelligence of man from the composition and elementary mixture of his bodily parts, heat and cold being the elements of things. The preponderant element characterises the thought of the individual man. But the chief legacy of Parmenides to his successors was his doctrine of the one immutable Being, which alone satisfies the requirements of an object of knowledge. The element of the Ionians did not satisfy these conditions, being endowed with the power to pass from one condition to another, whether intermittently or perpetually. Nothing, according to Parmenides, is ever generated or destroyed, however varied its manifestations and the changes it presents to the senses. On the foundation thus laid by Parmenides, Empedocles, Anaxagoras and Leucippus constructed their systems, resolving apparent generation and destruction into combination and separation of primary elements or principles, themselves indestructible. They differed, Aristotle remarks, as to the number and nature of these indestructible elements. Empedocles made a mistake in accepting a crude popular analysis into air, earth, fire and water, elements which do not so much as correspond to a rough division of matter into the solid, liquid and gaseous states. Anaxagoras, with his homoeomeries, was in our view still wider of the mark. Leucippus and Democritus at last found in the atoms a working hypothesis of the constitution of matter, which has lasted down to the present day. It is these three physical systems which most profoundly influenced Aristotle. He unfortunately accepted the first with modifications and opposed the last, by the merits of which he was nevertheless profoundly impressed. Each of these three systems took up the problem of the soul. But in the meantime medical enquiries had been actively prosecuted, and it is to a Pythagorean, Alcmaeon of Croton, that we owe the earliest advances towards the physiology of the senses. He was the first to recognise the brain as the central organ of intellectual activity. He dissected animals and by this means discovered the chief nerves of sense, which, like Aristotle, he called "conduits" or "channels," and he traced them to their termination in the brain. Deafness and blindness he held to be caused when by a concussion the brain was shifted out of its normal position and the channels of hearing and seeing respectively were thus blocked. He submitted the several senses to a searching examination, starting with the anatomical construction of the sense-organ. The air in the ear he regarded as a sounding-board, and he attributed to the moisture, softness, flexibility and warmth of the tongue its capacity to reduce solid bodies to fluid as a necessary preliminary to tasting. He noticed the phenomenon which we call seeing sparks when the eye has received a heavy blow, and this suggested a crude theory of vision, postulating fire in the eye, a mistake repeated by Empedocles and by Plato. But it is with the glittering or transparent element of water in the eye that it sees, and it sees better according to the purity of the element. Vision is effected by the image of the thing seen and by the rays which issue from the eye within and pass outwards through the water. He derived memory from sense-perception and opinion from memory; from memory and opinion combined he derived reason, which distinguishes men from the lower animals. What scanty information we have about him comes chiefly from Theophrastus, but it would be a great mistake to acquiesce in Aristotle's neglect of him. He is only once mentioned in *De Anima* as having held that soul is immortal, on the singular ground that by its incessant motion it resembles the heavenly bodies, which he also held to be immortal.

In Empedocles we are dealing not with a sober physical enquirer, but with a religious enthusiast and poet-philosopher. He accepted the transmigration of souls in a slightly altered form; he introduced wicked as well as good "daemons", condemned for their sins to wander for 10,000 years and to become souls of plants, beasts and men. In the course of their purification they become prophets, poets, physicians, princes, and again return to the gods. Sensation in general he explained by the action of like upon like. Particles emanate from external bodies and enter our bodies by channels or pores. They cannot enter unless there is a certain proportion between the emanation and the size and shape of the channel which is to receive it. Thus a sense-organ is a particular part of the body which, possessing channels of a certain size and shape, is adapted to receive emanations of a certain kind, of flavour, odour or sound. But his theory of vision was more complicated. Not only are there emanations from visible objects, but there are also emanations from the eye. To this he was led by the analogy of the dark lantern, of which the camera obscura furnishes a modern illustration. The transparent plates of horn or linen in the lantern, made to protect the flame from the wind which might otherwise extinguish it, correspond to the thin coats or films in the eye covering the pupil, whose contents are partly of a fiery, partly of a watery, nature. From the pupil fiery and watery emanations leap forth through funnel-shaped channels to meet the fiery and watery emanations coming, the one from light, the other from dark, objects outside. The principle of "like by like" accounts for the mutual attraction of similar materials and their meeting, and, when the two sets of emanations meet, vision takes place. The preponderance of water or fire in the eye accounts for the fact that some animals see better in the dark, others in the daylight. Thus, then, we perceive like by like, the four elements of all things, air, earth, fire and water, outside, because air, earth, fire and water are present in our bodies. Blood is the most perfect mixture of these four elements and to this blood where it is purest, viz. about the heart, he attributed thought. As we see earth by earth which is in us water by water, so we think by means of blood, the bodily tissue in which all four elements are most perfectly blended. Empedocles, then, consistently confined his attention to the bodily process. The mental or psychical state is either ignored in his explanation or reduced to its physical conditions. Yet on the problem of knowledge, aware of the imperfection of the senses, he counsels us to withdraw our trust from them and prefer the guidance of reason.

Anaxagoras distinguished sensation from intelligence and, whereas most of the Pre-Socratics agreed that we perceive things by having within us something like them, he held that we perceive in virtue of the presence within us of something opposite to the thing perceived. Knowledge is not to be gained from the senses, because their powers cannot discriminate minute changes; while the reactionary physics which he propounded involved the presence in every sensible object of infinitesimal particles perceptible only in the aggregate and, blended with these, alien particles altogether imperceptible, because infinitesimal. Over against this infinity of homoeomeries he set the other constituent of the universe, which alone is pure and unmixed and has nothing in common with anything else. This is Nous. The part it played was to communicate the first impulse to that rotatory motion which ultimately evolved from the chaos in which all things were mixed the present order and regularity of the universe. Nous is in all living beings, great and small, in varying degrees. It governs and orders and knows. We fortunately possess the account which Anaxagoras himself gave of Nous, and upon the evidence the reader must decide for himself what was its nature. Plato and Aristotle construed it as immaterial reason and censured the philosopher for not making more thoroughgoing use of its mighty agency. Returning now to sense, the contrast necessary to perception Anaxagoras found most clearly in touch, for our perception of temperature depends upon contrast. We know the taste of sweet and bitter only by contrast. Seeing, again, takes place by the reflection of an image in the pupil, but in a part of it which is of a different colour from the object seen. Eyes that see in the daytime are, generally speaking, dark, while animals with gleaming eyes see better by night.

In the Atomists the tendencies of earlier Greek thinkers reach mature development. The problem hitherto had been to determine what matter is, and Leucippus propounded a working hypothesis which has ever since been sufficient for the purposes of science. Though this theory is derived from sense, it departs very widely from the evidence of the senses. Knowledge, said Democritus, is of two kinds, genuine knowledge that there are atoms and void and nothing else, and knowledge which is dark or obscure, by which he meant the information given by the senses. The existence of void apparently contradicts observation, experiment fails even now to obtain an absolute void. The properties of body are all given by sense. The Atomists accepted the evidence of sense for resistance, extension and weight (perhaps Democritus was unaware of this last quality), but rejected it for colours, sounds, odours and flavours. Out of impenetrable atoms of different shapes and sizes the whole universe is built up, and the different qualities in things are due either to difference of shape or size, or to different arrangements, of the atoms composing them. The soul is no exception. It is a complex of atoms within the body. Soul-atoms are spherical in shape, extremely minute and mobile. They resemble the atoms of fire. In thus postulating a body within the body to account for vital and intellectual functions, Democritus reverts more consistently and systematically than any previous philosopher to the standpoint of the savage who, when he sees an animal move, is unable to explain the fact except by supposing that there is a little animal inside to move him. But there is this difference, that the little animal is imagined to be alive, the soul-atoms of Democritus are mere matter Thus to push the implicit assumptions of their predecessors to their logical consequences and make the half-conscious hylozoism of the early Ionians blossom forth in materialism is the great merit of Leucippus and Democritus. All processes of sensation, then, are instances of the contact between bodies. They are caused by "idols" or films which are constantly streaming off from the surface of bodies, of inconceivable thinness, yet preserving the relative shape of the parts. So far this agrees with Empedocles; but the latter made his emanations enter the body through channels, while the Atomists conceived them as entering by the void between the atoms. The same explanation would apply to thought, which is excited when the material image of an object enters the equally material mind. All the senses are thus but modifications of touch. This was made out satisfactorily for taste, and Democritus attempted to determine the shapes of the atoms which produce the different varieties of taste. Things made of atoms angular, winding, small and thin, have an acid taste, those whose atoms are spherical and not too small taste sweet, and so on. His four simple colours, white, black, red and green, are accounted for by the shape and disposition of atoms, but a similar analysts was not attempted for the objects of sound and smell. In marked contrast with the attempts which the Atomists and of even Empedocles made to bring physics and physiology into shape is the retrograde system of Diogenes of Apollonia, whose fantastic absurdities have been immortalised for us by Aristophanes, He was not satisfied with the resolution by Anaxagoras, himself a reactionary in physics, of bodies into infinitesimal particles possessing definite qualities, though he was more attracted by the supposition of unmixed Nous, which is the seat of intelligence. But he supplemented this theory by reverting to the position of the Ionians, one of whom, Anaximenes, had chosen air for his primary element. Diogenes endowed air with sentience and intelligence. "All creatures," he says, "live and see and hear by the same thing " (viz. air), "and from the same thing all derive their intelligence as well." He thus made the air in us play an important part in the processes of perception and thought. From Alcmaeon he must have borrowed the idea that the brain is the central organ; the air in the sense-organs, the eye, the ear, the nostrils, transmitted the impression to the air in or near the brain. The common view that seeing takes place by the reflection of an image in the pupil he supplemented by postulating that this image must be blended with the internal air; otherwise, though the image is formed, there is no seeing. He pointed to the fact that, when the optic nerve is inflamed, blindness ensues because, as he thought, the admixture with the internal air is prevented. His account of hearing may be cited for the likeness it bears to that given in *De Anima*. "The animals which hear most acutely have slender veins, the orifice of the ear (like that of the nose) being in them short, slender and straight, and the external ear erect and large. For movement of the air in the ears sets in motion the internal air" (in or near the brain). "Whereas, if the orifice be too wide, the movement of the air in the ears causes a ringing in them, and what is heard is indistinct noise, because the air upon which the audible sound impinges is not at rest."

In the fifth century the evolution of successive systems came to a halt. The progress of enquiry had been marked by the foundation of new sciences like geometry and astronomy, both in a flourishing condition, and new arts, like rhetoric and dialectic. The bustle and unrest of the times was attended by a growing mistrust, not only of the old traditional religious and moral beliefs, but of the bewildering intellectual movement which in so short a space of time had put forward so many brilliant and contradictory speculations. The professional educators, whom we know as the Sophists, turned as a rule to practical interests and made human ism, literary criticism, erudition their main themes. Protagoras, the greatest of them, adopted a sceptical attitude and maintained that man was the measure of all things, which, as interpreted by Plato, means that, as things appear to me, so they are to me, or the denial of objective truth. There were many sceptical currents in the sea of speculation on which Greece had embarked. The followers of Heraclitus pushed the doctrine of flux to an extreme. Things never are, but are always becoming, they have no fixed attributes. When we say that a thing is, we must in the same breath pronounce that it is not. There are always two of these fluxes, one the movement or change producing sensations, flux outside, the other the movement which receives the sensations, the flux of our senses. The result of the contact between them is that, for example, wood becomes white wood and the eye becomes a seeing eye. When the flux of Socrates well comes in contact with wine, the wine will be sweet, but, if he is ill, it will be sour. Both these statements will be true: in fact, all statements are true. What wine is depends entirely on the man perceiving it. There is no criterion of truth in external things, they change so rapidly. On the other hand, Gorgias of Leontini in his essay on Nature or the Non-existent hardly caricatured the position of the younger Eleatics when he put forward the thesis that, if anything existed, it could not be known, and, if anything did exist and was known, it could not be communicated. Such views as these or that of Euthydemus that falsehood is impossible are by no means universal among the Sophists, many of whom had no psychological or epistimological theories at all; and, where their views were sceptical, it was the scepticism not of one school, but of many. Aristotle justifies the revolt of the Sophists against philosophy, he holds that most of the leading Pre-Socratic systems tend implicitly or explicitly to the doctrine of Protagoras. Protagoras first called attention to the importance of the knowing mind in every act of knowledge. In the view of a plain man like Socrates all the systems were discredited and the question, what is knowledge, was for the time more urgent than the ambitious problems proposed by those who had sought to know the nature of the universe. Psychology can glean nothing from the ethical discussions of the historical Socrates. When he declared that virtue is knowledge, he was confessedly using the latter term as one which neither he nor his interlocutors could adequately define.

Plato in his writings is always talking about the soul, but not all that he says is intended to be taken seriously. We must allow for the mythical element, and in particular for his imaginative sympathy with the whole mass of floating legend, myth and dogma, of a partly religious, partly ethical character, which, as was stated above, found a wide but not universal acceptance at an early time in the Orphic and Pythagorean associations and brotherhoods. The Platonic myths afford ample evidence that Plato was perfectly familiar with all the leading features of this strange creed. The divine origin of the soul, its fall from bliss and from the society of the gods, its long pilgrimage of penance through hundreds of generations, its task of purification from earthly pollution, its reincarnations in successive bodies, its upward or downward progress, and the law of retribution for all offences, these and kindred subjects the fancy of Plato has embellished with all the beauty and sublimity which the art of a lost poet could bestow upon prose. Such themes stir his imagination. His approval of ethical fiction is attested by his own words, but it would be the height of imprudence to infer that any part of his philosophy is bound up with his gorgeous poetical imagery, Plato never set about writing a treatise *De Anima*. We find anticipations of a science, but not the science itself. In each dialogue he has a particular end in view. He proposes to examine the doctrine of Protagoras or, it may be, the import of predication. Incidentally in the course of a long controversy we come across models of psychological analysis which for subtlety and insight have never been equalled. Such an analysis was something absolutely new. The psychical or mental states on which Plato fixed his attention had hitherto, when they were not ignored altogether, been confounded with their bodily concomitants: a mistake not unnatural, so long as both sensation and thought were regard cil as changes in the body. In the *Theaetetus* we find the following argument. We do not perceive by but through the senses. What we perceive through one sense we cannot perceive through another. Consequently, if we know something about both a sound and a colour, it cannot be known through sense. Now we do know many such things; that they are, that they are different from one another, that both are two things and that each is one. How do we know such facts? The soul apprehends them through itself without any sense-organs. Being and Not-Being, likeness and unlikeness, number, identity and diversity are not apprehended through sense, but through the soul alone. The soul apprehends the noble and the base, the good and the bad, not through the senses, but by calculating in herself the past or present in relation to the future. All men and animals from the moment of birth have by nature sensations which pass through the body and reach the soul, but to compare these sensations in relation to Being and expediency comes with difficulty and requires a long time, much trouble and education. It is impossible to attain truth and know it without attaining Being; knowledge does not consist in affections of sense because we cannot by them attain Being. It is by reasoning about sensations that this is alone possible.

In the *Phaedo* the Platonic Socrates undertakes to prove that learning is reminiscence, which indeed is implied by the fact that, if questions are properly put, the right answers are elicited, showing that the knowledge sought, the knowledge, e.g. of geometry, existed previously in the mind of the respondent. This proof is as follows. The picture of a lyre reminds us of the person who used the lyre, a picture of Simmias may remind us of Kebes or of Simmias himself, so that the reminiscence may be brought about either indirectly or directly. If it is effected directly and the object seen is similar to the object it recalls, we cannot fail to see how far the remembrance is exact For instance, we affirm that there is an idea of equality which is called to our minds by our perception of sensibles which are equal That this idea is something distinct from the equal sensibles is clear; for the sensibles may appear equal to one observer, unequal to another; but about the idea of equality no difference of opinion is possible. Now we are to observe that all sensible equals appear to us as falling short of the standard of absolute equality, which plainly shows that our knowledge of absolute equality is prior to our perception of the sensibles. And whereas this sense of deficiency in the sensiblees has been present so long as we have had any perceptions of them, our perceptions of them date from the moment of our birth, it inevitably follows that our knowledge of the idea must have been acquired before our birth. Now this of course applies to all ideas as well as to that of equality. Since, then, we have obtained this knowledge, two alternatives are open: either we are born in full possession of it and retain it through life, or we lose it at birth and gradually regain it. The first must be dismissed on this ground: if a man knows a thing, he can give an account of it, but we see that men cannot give an account of the ideas; it follows then that the second alternative is true; we lose this knowledge and all learning is but the recovery of it. And since our souls certainly did not acquire it during their human life, they must have gained it before our birth and at birth lost it. Many more passages might be cited to prove that Plato kept the mental process distinct from the bodily process and that it is the former which he sought to explain.

Though the various mental operations are often discussed and distinguished, yet we find no exhaustive classification in any dialogue. The reason is obvious. The variation is due to the fact that each attempt at partial classification is made, as above stated, for a special purpose, to prove a particular conclusion in a particular dialogue. Thus in the *Republic* the tripartite division into reason, passion and appetite is brought in to show the relation of justice to the other virtues, and this, again, whether subordinate to, or coordinate with, the analogy between the individual and the state, is a means to the determination of a perfect political constitution, which is said in the *Timaeus* to have been the chief subject of the dialogue. Nor does this tripartite division itself tally either with that into knowledge, opinion (or sense-presentation) and ignorance, or again, with the fourfold division into thinking, understanding, belief and conjecture (an expansion probably of the distinction between knowledge and opinion), which we find in other parts of the *Republic*. In the *Sophist* discursive thought is a dialogue of the soul with herself, opinion is the silent assertion of the soul in which this results, imagining is a combination of opinion and sensation. In the *Philebus* Plato goes more into detail and distinguishes sensation, memory, imagination and recollection. When the affections of the body do not reach the soul, the state of the soul is said to be insensibility or unconsciousness. When the affections of the body are communicated through the body to the soul, there is sensation. The retention of such a sensation is memory, its non-retention, the fading of memory, is forgetfulness. The recovery of lost memories by the soul without the aid of the body is recollection. Later in the dialogue the relation of memory to imagination is illustrated: the former is a scribe or recorder, what it records being propositions, opinions; the latter is a painter, whose glowing pictures excite hope. In this dialogue also there is a practical end, all these distinctions being subservient to the classification of pleasures as true or false. Similarly in a memorable passage of the *Theaetetus* the introduction of two illustrations, one from a waxen block and the other from a dovecot or aviary, is incidental to a refutation of the thesis that knowledge is true opinion. But the similes in themselves are contributions to psychology of permanent value. That of the waxen block presents in its sum and substance the entire theory of sensation conceived as an impression from without, like the print of a seal upon wax, and the theory of memory as the retention of such impressions, the different degrees of retentiveness in individuals being ascribed to the size of the block, the quality of the wax and the number of impressions crowded together in small compass. The other, that of the aviary, conveys in a striking manner the relation between memory and reminiscence, the latter being the deliberate recovery of lost impressions; at the same time it shows the relation between the mere possession of knowledge and its actual application or exercise.

The most comprehensive view of Plato's psychology is to be found in the *Timaeus*. He starts with reason or with the operations of intellect. The soul thinks. This process is first described as it goes on in the soul of the universe or universal soul and, because it is an activity, is compared with circular motion. The revolution of two circles, that of the Same and that of the Other, gives judgments of identity and difference, the two most important relations, and without such judgements there can be no knowledge. But this ceaseless activity of thought from time to time suffers disturbance, and the interference results in sensation. In the allegory the creation of particular souls follows upon the creation of universal soul, and it is to these particular souls, each united to a body, that the following description applies. When the revolutions of the immortal soul had thus been confined in a body, a body, as Plato says, "in-flowing and out-flowing continually," these revolutions, "being confined in a great river, neither controlled it nor were controlled, but bore and were borne violently to and fro. For great as was the tide sweeping over them and flowing off which brought them sustenance, a yet greater tumult was caused by the effects of the bodies that struck against them; as when the body of any one came in contact with some alien fire that met it from without, or with solid earth, or with liquid glidings of water, or if he were caught in a tempest of winds borne on the air." The body of the animal, be it remembered, is composed of the same four elements, air, earth, fire, water, with which the animal comes in contact in alien bodies, whether in the process of nutrition or in that of sensation. "And so the motions from all these elements rushing through the body penetrated to the soul. This is in fact the reason why these have all alike been called and still are called sensations. Then too did they produce the most wide and vehement agitation for the time being, joining with the perpetually streaming current in stirring and violently shaking the revolutions of the soul, so that they altogether hindered the circle of the Same by flowing contrary to it, and they stopped it from governing and from going; while the circle of the Other they displaced.... So that the circles can barely hold to one another, and though they are in motion, it is motion without law, sometimes reversed, now slanting, and now inverted.... And when from external objects there meets them anything that belongs to the class of the Same or to that of the Other, then they declare its relative sameness or difference quite contrariwise to the truth, and show themselves false and irrational; and no circuit is governor or leader in them at that time. And whenever sensations from without rushing up and falling upon them drag along with them the whole vessel of the soul, then the circuits seem to govern though they really are governed. On account then of all these experiences the soul is at first bereft of reason, now as in the beginning, when she is confined in a mortal body." The soul, according to this account, is in ceaseless activity, and such normal activity, or thought, is from time to time disturbed by sensation, which has a tendency to pervert right thinking into falsehood and error. We might compare the definition from the *Philebus* above summarised, in which it is said that when the bodily affections pass through both body and soul and give rise there to a sort of shock or tremor not only peculiar to each, but shared by both in common, the movement which body and soul thus share may properly be called sensation.

Plato started with intellect and thought. Rightly understood, he does not oppose body to soul, but rather sense to reason, as one faculty of soul to another. But what are the limits of sense and reason? To which should be referred the knowledge of relations of cause and effect, of good and evil? Sense, we are told in the Republic, is sufficient where a thing does not tend to pass into or be confused with its opposite; where the data tend to become confused, sense is insufficient and we must appeal to intellect. What sense perceives confusedly thought thinks distinctly and in isolation. Sense at the best can only give opinion, but reason and true opinion are distinct "because they are different in origin and unlike in nature. The one is engendered in us by instruction, the other by persuasion; the one is ever accompanied by right understanding, the other is without understanding; the one is not to be moved by persuasion, the other yields to persuasion; true opinion we must admit is shared by all men, but reason by the gods alone and a very small portion of mankind." Sense and thought are concerned with different objects, the particular and the universal. The defects of sense are not in the subject, but in the object, because the particulars of sense are in flux and have no fixed being. Prota- goras held that sensible things have their so-called qualities only by acting or being acted upon and, as activity and passivity are always relative, no quality belongs to any thing *per se*. We cannot say that they are *per se* anything in particular, or even that they are at all. They only become: things are always becoming, not being. When an object comes in contact with our scnse-organ and interaction takes place, a sensation arises in the organ and simultaneously the object becomes possessed of a certain quality. But the sensation in the organ and the quality in the object are results which are produced only by the contact and last only as long as it lasts. In this doctrine of Heraclitus and Protagoras Plato acquiesced, so far as it relates to sense and sensibles. The testimony of Aristotle on this point is explicit and the dialogues confirm it But, instead of concluding with Protagoras that all presentations are relatively true and that there is no such thing as objective truth, he drew a different inference, viz. that, if there is such a thing as knowledge, which he firmly believed, its object must be an intelligible object and an universal.

The process of sensation in the separate bodily organs is thus described in the *Timaeus*. "When that which is naturally mobile is impressed by ever such a slight affection, it spreads abroad the motion, the particles one upon another producing the same effect, until, coming to that which is conscious, it announces the property of the agent: but a substance that is immobile is too stable to spread the motion round about, and thus merely receives the affection, but does not stir any neighbouring part; so that, as the particles do not pass on one to another the original impulse which affected them, they keep it untransmitted to the entire creature and thus leave the recipient of the affection without sensation. This takes place with our bones and hair and all the parts we have which are formed mostly of earth: while the former conditions apply in the highest degree to sight and hearing, because they contain the greatest proportion of fire and air." For the process of vision Plato adopts with modifications the theory of Empedocles, for the process of hearing that of the Pythagoreans. As to smell, he holds that odours cannot be classified according to kinds. For no element in its normal state can be perceived by smell, because the vessels of the nostrils are too narrow to admit water or earth and too wide to be excited by air or fire. They can thus only perceive an element in process of dissolution, when it is being liquefied or decomposed or dissolved or evaporated. The object of smell, then, is either vapour, which is water changing to air, or mist, which is air changing to water. The only classification we can make is that scents which disturb the substance of the nostrils are unpleasant, while those which restore the natural state are pleasant. In his account of tasting Plato makes the sensation depend upon the contraction or dilatation of the pores of the tongue by substances that are dissolved in the mouth, the peculiar effect of the principal flavours being briefly indicated. He

20

made the flesh the organ of touch and, considering the various tactile sensations as relative to the tangibles, proceeds to explain what constitutes bodies hot and cold, hard and soft, heavy and light.

I have dwelt at what some may think inordinate length upon Plato, because in psychology, as elsewhere, making allowance for the fundamental difference between the two philosophers, we find nothing in Aristotle but the development in a systematic form of the Platonic heritage. It was the disciple's task to maintain on independent grounds the essentials of the master's doctrine on the subject of the soul, and to do this in the face of the widely conflicting views and the general uncertainty which, as the foregoing sketch sufficiently shows, were prevalent at the time. With the conscious or half-conscious materialism of his predecessors Aristotle has no more sympathy than Plato and, as compared with this point of agreement, the differences between them count for little, however much Aristotle may exaggerate them. In the criticism which he passes upon the *Timaeus* he affects to take the narrative literally. The point at issue is whether the activity which both Plato and Aristotle ascribe to the thinking soul can justly and reasonably be called a movement The doctrine of the two philosophers is on all important points the same: they agree that there is an immortal soul and a mortal soul, that the immortal element thinks always and that thinking must belong to its essence. What Plato calls "movement" is familiar enough in Aristotle as "energy"' or "activity". If Plato would only say "energy", there would seemingly be no room for objection. But in the tenth book of the *Laws*, the work of his old age, when he may have been presumed to have had some acquaintance with the views of his desciple, Plato obdurately refused to say "energy," and by his classification of the ten species of motion assimilated physical movement and change to the only activity which in his view had reality, the, "movement" of thought, defining the soul as that which is able to move itself. And after his death Xenocrates persisted in attributing "movement" to the number which is the soul. At this point a brief summary of the first part of Aristotle's treatise may be the best means of indicating the way in which the writer approaches his subject and the conclusions at which he arrives.

Book I

At the outset, he says, we wish to ascertain the nature or substance, and the accidents, of the soul, which is a principle of animal life. A few preliminary enquiries are suggested. Is soul "something"? Substance? Or quality? Or to which category does it belong? Is it potentially existent or is it an actuality? Is it divisible or without parts? This suggests the further question, Is it homogeneous in all species of animals? If not, are the differences between souls generic or specific differences? If it is without parts, it must be variable, there will be many sorts of soul. If it is homogeneous, the homogeneous soul must be made up of different parts. Ought we, then, to start with the whole soul or with the parts, ought we to study the parts first or their functions, and, if the functions, why not first the objects? As an apology for not deciding, it may be remarked that, while in order to know the properties of a thing, we ought to know its essence, yet knowledge of properties contributes to knowledge of essence: in fact, the one is involved in the other.

The attributes of the soul cannot properly be separated from those of the body. The one that seems most separable is thinking: but, if this is akin to imagining or if it involves an image, neither is thinking separable. If any attribute is peculiar to the soul itself, then soul may be independent of body; if not, soul cannot be so independent. The attributes of soul are notions or forms in matter and, as such, fall within the province of the physicist or natural philosopher, while the dialectician studies and defines their form apart from their matter. Here is the point of difference between the objects of physics and of mathematics: the attributes of soul as such, e.g. fear and anger, are inseparable from the physical matter of the animals to which they belong; the mathematical objects, e.g. line and surface, though really inseparable, are separable in thought from the concrete things to which they belong.

From this discussion of method we pass to consider the opinions of our predecessors. The characteristics of animate being are motion and sensation. Hence some have regarded the soul as *par excellence* the cause of motion, Democritus, who thought it fire, and Anaxagoras, being typical instances. All assumed that if a thing causes motion, it is itself moved. Others, again, start with the assumption that like is known by like and infer that the soul is composed of all the elements, whether they are one or many: Empedocles that it is composed of earth, air, fire and water; Plato of number. All definitions maybe reduced to three: that it causes motion, is perceptive, is incorporeal. The last characteristic leads those to choose the finest matter, who acknowledge none but corporeal elements. Subsequently it is objected that if the soul is a fine matter, as the soul is in all the sensitive body, we have two bodies in one.

The application of the idea of motion to the soul leads, it is argued, to absurdities. There are four kinds of motion, locomotion, qualitative change, decay, growth, and our enquiry is whether the soul is moved in and through itself, and not as sailors in a ship. All kinds of motion are in space; therefore, if the soul is moved, the soul must be in space. As it moves the body, it would naturally move like the body; and in that case it would up and down in, and in and out of, the body. In general, we contend, the soul does not move the body, as Democritus supposed, by physical agency, but by means of purpose of some sort, that is, thought. The most thorough application of motion to explain soul, and in particular the soul which thinks, was made by Plato in the *Timaeus*, and this is criticised at some length. Like other theories, it neglects the relation between soul and body in virtue of which the soul acts, the body is acted upon, the soul moves and the body is moved.

Another definition of the soul makes it a harmony or blending of opposites. This notion may be applicable to health or any bodily excellence, but will not apply to the soul. Harmony will not cause motion. Harmony means either (1) a close fit or adjustment of bodies, or (2) the proportion in which elements are mixed. It is needless to show that the first meaning is inapplicable, there are so many fittings of the limbs. As to (2) in flesh and blood the elements are mixed in different proportions; which mixture is the soul? Returning to motion, we conclude that the only motion of which soul admits is motion *per accidens,* due to motion of the body, as whiteness is moved when a white body is moved. A stronger argument than any our predecessors have adduced is derived from the attributes of the soul, such as pain and pleasure, fear, anger, and other emotions, sensation and thought, all of which are commonly believed to be movements. In them, however, the soul is not moved: it is merely the cause of movement in the heart or some other bodily part. It would be better to ascribe these attributes to the man and say that he perceives or thinks or feels pleasure and pain with his soul. This leads to an interesting digression on intellect, followed by a refutation of Xenocrates, who defined the soul as a self-moving number. How can the attributes which are known to belong to soul possibly be deduced from such a definition? It will not afford even the slightest hint of them. The same argument had previously been used against the definition of soul as a harmony.

Two characteristics of soul, (1) that it moves itself, (2) that it is composed of very fine matter, have now been dismissed. Against the third, that it is composed of the elements and that like knows like, it may be urged that then the soul ought to have in it all compounds, all categories. Moreover, a unifying principle would be needed. The soul is not to be held divisible into parts independent of each other, for in that case what keeps its parts together ? That must be the real soul. Again, as the whole soul keeps the whole body together, each part of the soul should keep a part of the body together: but we can assign no such function to intellect.

Book II

Book II begins by defining the soul. We premise that of entities to which categories are applied substance is one, where by substance we mean either (1) matter, which is not yet anything in particular, or (2) form, which makes it something in particular, or (3) the union of matter and form in the particular thing. Under substance in the last sense is included a natural body partaking of life. What we mean by life is the power of the body to nourish itself and to grow and decay of itself. Body is clearly matter here, therefore soul is form. And, if for matter and form we substitute potentiality and actuality and distinguish the first stage of actuality, corresponding to knowledge, from the second, corresponding to the exercise of knowledge, the soul will be the first actuality of a natural body furnished with organs, or of a body that has in itself the principle of movement and rest. Thus soul is the quiddity or formal essence, to which we have analogies in the cutting power of the axe and the visual power of the eye, both actualities in the first degree, as contrasted with actual cutting and actual seeing, which are actualities in the second degree.

The definition thus found is the most comprehensive possible, applying to life in all its various forms, (1) intellect, (2) sense, (3) locomotion, (4) motion of nutrition, growth and decay. Plants exhibit life in its last form only. Animals, in addition to this, have sensation. Of the different senses touch is indispensable. Experiment shows that most of these vital functions are really inseparable from one another, though at the same time separable in thought. Whether this holds of intellect also it is not so easy to decide. If to these vital functions be added appetence, which clearly is present where sensation is, a certain gradation can be recognised. They may be arranged in an ascending series. The lower can exist without the higher, but the higher in mortal creatures always involve the lower. And there is a similar gradation in the senses. It seems, then, that there is one definition of soul exactly as there is one definition of rectilinear figure. Alike in figures and in the various types of soul, the earlier members of the series exist implicitly and potentially in the later; the triangle is implicit in the quadrilateral and the nutritive faculty in the sensitive. The definition does not dispense us from investigating in detail what is the soul in the plant, in the brute, and in man.

Having reached this point, we naturally expect that each of the four main vital functions, nutrition, sensation, intellect, locomotion, will be investigated in detail; and this in fact is what the writer proceeds to do. Nutrition, growth and decay and reproduction are dealt with briefly in Book II, Ch. 4; sense-perception at very great length, Book II, Ch. 5; Book III, Ch. 2; and imagination, which is intimately connected with sense, in Book III, Ch. 3; upon imagination follows intellect, Book III, Chs. 4-8; and, lastly, the principle of progressive motion in animals, which is identified with appetence, occupies us in Book III, Chs. 9-11. The treatise ends with an attempt, from the standpoint of teleology, to answer the question why the various forms of life occur in this ascending scale.

Aristotle himself was not consciously constructing a new science. His discussion of the soul was forced upon him when, traversing the wide domain he had set apart for his science of nature or physics, he passed from inorganic to the borders of organic life. The method of science laid down in the *Organon*, and hitherto pursued, is a method partly inductive, partly deductive, aiming to establish rational theories on empirical data and often falling short of its aim, because either the data were at fault or the theories inappropriate, or because there were defects in both. Natural science has to do with nature and with natural bodies, which by common consent are pre-eminently substances, sensible substances. Nature is itself a cause of things, the power in the things themselves which makes them whnt they are. Its characteristic is that, like human intelligence, it devises means to ends. In this respect natural bodies or natural substances may be compared with the products of art and skill, but in the former case the cause is, and in the latter case is not, in the product itself. We wish to know what are (1) the concrete natural substances, (2) their properties, (3) their physical changes, (4) the causes of these changes. If we could answer these questions, we should know the ends of nature in making concrete substances, the means used to realise these ends, the form and matter of which the substances consist. In logic we proceed from one determination to another. Psychology is concerned with mental acts or operations. In some of these operations we are conscious of a process; for example, in operations of reason we know how we reason, by what steps we advance. To seareh for a method is to aim at determining the order and arrangement in which these processes follow one another in any science. In geometry certain principles are assumed and necessary conclusions are deduced from them. Induction generalises from known particulars in order to obtain principles. Both induction and deduction may be combined in a more comprehensive method which, after establishing general principles, deduces derivative laws and verifies the particular conclusions which follow from them. But it may be impossible to apply this complete method directly in its simplicity. The effects, which are conclusions, may be known, while the causes are to seek. If so, it is necessary to infer backwards and discover the causes from the effects. The early progress of mathematics and astronomy, with their applications to optics and harmonics, led to the belief, which Plato endorses, that deduction is the method of scientific researeh. Aristotle agreed for pure mathematics, while in applied mathematics he regarded induction from the materials collected as, strictly speaking, lying outside of the science and subsidiary. But in the natural sciences, where we rise from effects to causes, a thorough description of facts is a necessary preliminary to the discovery of the ultimate principles, and the inverse method must be applied. The method of astronomy, we are told, was to collect the facts, the phenomena, and from them to deduce astronomical laws. The whole method is summed up with convenient brevity thus "In every department of nature we must first ascertain the facts and then after that state the causes." The task to which the *History of Animals* is devoted is thus described: "First let us ascertain the existing varieties of animals and the properties of each, and after that we must try to discover their causes. This is the natural method which puts the collection of material first. Characteristic of Aristotle's mind is the notion that some things can be got at both deductively and inductively: it is the consilience of fact and theory. The soul being a part of nature, psychology must needs be a branch of general physics, as all preceding thinkers, including Plato, agreed. The presuppositions of Aristotle's metaphysics refer life to a cause. Vital phenomena, wherever found, are sufficiently alike in their manifestations to justify the assumption of one such cause. The treatise, then, is a preamble to all parts of the system dealing with plants, or animals, or with yet higher beings, if endowed with life. As one of the series of biological works, it stands in the closest connexion with the tracts known as the *Parva Naturalia*, with the morphological treat*ise De Partibus Animalium*, and with that upon embryology, *De Generatione Animalium*. The part which the enquirer professes to take calls for very careful demareation. It is impossible tn say what contributions, if any, Aristotle himself made in the field of psychology: the presumption is that they were but small. The evidence of his dependence upon Plato for all that relates to psychical phenomena is so overwhelming, so constant. Possibly the repeated illustrations from zoophytes or stationary animals and from worms, which give signs of life after they have been severed into parts, are original; but in the main his facts are precisely the facts of his predecessors, the scantiest stock now at the disposal of any ignorant layman. Speculation had outrun observation. Nor is there any complaint of the scantiness of the data. No. Such as they are, they have already called forth too numerous and too divergent explanations. The writer's modest aim is by preliminary discussion to settle a few, just a few, fundamental questions as to the nature and attributes of the one principle of life and mind.

Aristotle's enquiry is founded on his metaphysics. It is the business of natural science to discover form and matter in natural substances. Every animal, every plant is a natural substance, compounded of body, which is matter, and soul, which is form, and the science of nature has therefore to investigate both body and soul. Yet here a proviso is needed. Natural science does not necessarily treat of the whole soul. Wherever soul as form is in matter, wherever it employs a bodily organ, we are still in the domain of natural science; but anything included under soul which is independent of the body and which cannot be thus defined must be reserved for metaphysics. The meaning which Aristotle attached to independence or separate existence must be grasped, if we would understand what he conceived by a substance or thing. Primarily this separate existence is the attribute of concrete particulars presented to sense in the external world. They are bodies locally, numerically and by magnitude separate. From them the conception is transferred to whatever the mind thinks as distinct, and even for immaterial notions Aristotle has no other formula. They, too, like concrete bodies, are described as being in time, in space and in conception separate or distinct. In reducing soul to the logical essence or form of body Aristotle, according to his own presuppositions, so far from favouring materialism, secures once and for all the soul's absolute immateriality. The living body has independent existence, has its own form and its own matter. Even a dead body or an inanimate thing is something existing independently, to which we can apply the pronoun "this". But the soul does not exist in the same way. Nor, again, is it a thing capable of being added to or subtracted from another thing, the body, any more than form in general is a thing which can in mechanical fashion be united to and separated from its appropriate matter. If a brazen sphere be melted down, the brass remains. It is still "this" something, "this" mass of metal; but we cannot then say of its spherical shape that it is " this" anything or that it any longer exists. The lifeless body is like the eye which cannot see or the axe which is spoilt for use. We may apply to them the same names as before; but, as the nature is no longer the same, the application is irrelevant, misleading, equivocal. But, though the lifeless body is still a concrete particular and a substance, the soul apart from its relation to the body is no such thing at all. Now the soul as form stands to the body as matter of the concrete individual precisely as the spherical shape to the brass, as vision to the eye, as cutting power to the axe. In every case the form is a quality predicable of the matter. But the body is not predicable of the soul, we cannot explain the soul in terms of body or make it a material thing, however fine the materials. On the contrary, we must explain body in terms of soul. It is form which determines and we only know a thing as determined. Primary matter, the absolutely indeterminate, is in itself unknowable. Therefore, if we would know the living body, we must study its activities and operations and all the attributes which it acquires in virtue of soul. Soul and body, then, are not two distinct things, they are one thing presenting two distinct aspects. The soul is not body, but belongs to body; it is not itself a concrete particular, although its presence in the body makes a concrete particular; it resides in a body and, what is more, in a body of a particular kind, furnished with the means whereby the functions of the soul can be exercised. The relation of matter to form in the particular thing is one instance of a relation of higher generality, that between potence and act, between the power to become and the realisation of that power in actuality. Before it is, a thing may be or may not be, and when it is, if it has the power to act, it may act or it may not act. Now body stands to soul, and matter to form in general, as the potential to the actual which has reached the first stage and already is. In other words, the soul is the power which the living body possesses and the lifeless body lacks. This is first actualisation or first entelechy. Again, the actual possession of faculties unused still stands to the exercise of these faculties in the relation of potence to act. Life itself, the use of actual power, is the second stage, energy. The actual use must be prrccdrel by actual power. Soul is actual power to live but is not life. In Plato body is opposed to soul. The body could be trained to obey the soul by gymnastic and music. In Aristotle the body is the natural instrument of the soul, and so the body into which a particular soul enters must be adapted to its use. This fact renders the Pythagorean idea of transmigration absurd. Soul is likewise both the final and efficient cause of the body. It is the final cause, because the soul is merely means to vital power and life; it is the efficient cause not only in the obvious case of progressive motion, but also in all the various changes which the body undergoes in the exercise of vital functions, including nutrition, growth, sensation.

Such, in brief, is the description of soul considered in and by itself, including the various separate powers, which are assumed to account for the varieties of vital and psychical operations. The great problem is how this multiplicity of acts or operations should be classified. Plato in some dialogues divides soul into parts, an immortal part, reason, and two mortal parts, passion and appetite. His pupil is more cautious. He does not go beyond the supposition of certain powers or faculties. In one sense, he says, this division into powers is illusory, for the powers of soul are really infinite in number. But he contends that his own groups are convenient groups. Faculties, like every other basis of classification, are only means to an end. Plato, he thinks, should have added the nutritive and sensitive faculties. Desire, again, runs through all operations: there is the rational wish, the angry impulse and the instinctive appetite. Here at least it is clear that the different powers are but different capacities of the single soul. Yet his ignorance of the bodily conditions of thought and his consequent assumption of a separable and immortal part of soul leave Aristotle much in the same position as Plato. In order to get a clear view, special stress must be laid upon the statement that the powers of soul are arranged in an ascending scale. In mortal creatures, at all events, the higher faculty always presupposes the lower, without which it cannot exist. The lowest power, that of nutrition and propagation, is common to animals with plants; in plants it exists alone. Animals have sensitivity in addition: of the senses they must possess at least touch. So far we are on safe ground. From this point we may simplify in one of two ways. In the third Book the two faculties, sense and intellect, tend more and more to be conjoined as the judging faculty, while appetency, which in its lowest form is implied by sense, is made the principle on which progressive motion depends. These considerations lead to the following scheme:

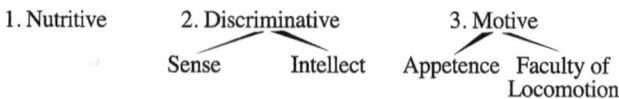

1. Nutritive	2. Discriminative		3. Motive	
	Sense	Intellect	Appetence	Faculty of Locomotion

28

On the other hand, intellect is said to be the highest of all our powers, and the lower forms of appetency, as well as the power of progressive motion, are associated with sense, while an intermediate place must be found for the imaginative faculty. These considerations suggest the following table of faculties:

1. Nutritive; 2. Sensitive, which is also appetitive; (this is in most animals joined with) 3. Locomotive; 4. Imaginative; 5. Intellective.

In the ascending series of vital functions we start with the lowest, which constitute the sole life of plants and are an indispensable element in the life of animals. Their isolation from all others in the vegetable kingdom facilitates their study. We accordingly assume a power of self-nourishment, the nutritive faculty. But we must be careful to remember that this faculty has also to account for growth, decay and reproduction; by which last it partakes, so far as it can, of immortality, the species of plants, as well as of animals, being imperishable, though the individual members of the species perish. If we are to define things by their end, the primary soul, the soul of the plant, is that which is capable of reproducing the species. But if the individual plant or animal is to be capable of this, it must be kept alive. Hence in a certain sense the subsidiary functions of nourishment and growth are even more important than the end to which they are means. Food or nutriment is the correlative object of the nutritive faculty, and we must determine how, things are nourished. It was a common opinion that contraries are nourished by contraries. This is generally, but not always, true of the elements or simple bodies. Fire, Aristotle points out, is nourished by water, but not water by fire. Others said like was nourished by like. These two views can be reconciled. Undigested food is unlike, but food, when digested, has been assimilated to that which it nourishes, and then like is nourished by like. Nutrition, then, is motion or change, and it is easy to discover the movent, the instrument and the moved. Soul is the nourisher, food the instrument of nutrition, body the nourished. Vital heat, as well as food, is employed by the soul in the process, and we have an analogy in the steersman, who employs his hand to move the rudder with which he steers the ship.

Little suspecting what advances botanical science was to make, Aristotle denied that plants have sensitivity. He admits that they are affected by heat and cold, but only, he argues, as inanimate things are affected; that is, they are simply heated and cooled. They cannot receive the form of objects without the matter, and this because they have no organ in which the elements are so blended as to give the means of discriminating, say, cold and heat. When a plant touches an object, there is merely physical contact. Thus the excessive preponderance, as Aristotle supposed, of "earth" in the structure of plants precludes sensation, because it precludes the proper blending of the elements, which would be necessary to make organs of sense. The insensibility of certain tissues of the body, e.g. bones, sinews, hair, he explained in a similar way as due to the presence in them of too much earth: and in this erroneous view he followed Plato.

The characteristic of animals when contrasted with plants is that they not only live, but have the power to perceive, which the Greeks regarded as essentially a cognitive power. They thought that we cannot perceive by sense without perceiving something, and interpreted this something objectively, as something which exists. The distinction so important for modern psychology between sensation and perception had not yet received much attention. For Aristotle, as for his predecessors, the main question is, in what does this operation of perceiving consist and how does it take place? We must describe the various kinds of perception and determine how perceiving is related to thinking, since both are cognitive. One distinctive mark in that by sense we perceive individuals. But we have much knowledge of individuals which the five senses cannot give. Does, then, all this knowledge come from sense, or must it be referred in part to intellect, or must we invent new faculties or powers to account for it? Suffice it to say that, whenever perception takes place, an universal is perceived, but not directly and *per se*, only *per accidens*. Directly sense perceives only "this", just as directly sense perceives it here and now. The operation of perceiving something existent is made by Aristotle to depend on his own physical theories of motion, of efficient cause and of essential form. One species of motion he defines as the production of an effect in matter by an efficient cause, as, e.g., the production of an impression upon wax by a seal or of an image in a mirror by a candle. Motions may be classified according to the categories as qualitative, quantitative or spatial, and the species of motion to which sense-perception is referred is the first species or qualitative change, the alteration or transformation which a thing undergoes when it loses certain qualities and acquires new ones, remaining itself numerically the same. The form or essence without the matter is transmitted by the efficient cause or agent to the patient upon whom it acts, as when fire transmits heat to fuel. The form or essence is one in all the things thus affected. The one universal heat is the same wherever actually found, in fuel ignited, in water heated or in molten iron. Applying this physical theory, we should define the particular motion or qualitative change which we call perceiving by sense as the production of an effect in a particular part of the body, which we call a sense-organ, by a particular external thing, which we call the sensible object. But this is inadequate. Plants receive heat and cold and the air receives odour, but they do not perceive. It is not enough, then, to say that perceiving is undergoing some affection or being acted upon. Besides, what is affected? Not the single organ, but the percipient as a whole and we have seen that the animal is a particular case of composite substance, the body being matter, the sentient soul form. Now it is with the soul that we perceive, as it is with the soul that we live and think. Let us, then, amend the definition. Perception is an alteration in the soul. It consists in the production by an external object of an effect in the sensitive faculty. This effect is the reception of the form, without the matter, of the external thing perceived.

Thus Aristotle is able to decide between the conflicting views of his predecessors, according to some of whom like acts upon like, while Heraclitus and Anaxagoras insisted that for any change to be perceived object and percipient must be unlike. As we saw about nutrition, both are right and both are wrong. The *percipiendum* is unlike, the *perceptum* is like, that which perceives it, for, when the process of perceiving takes place, both the external thing which causes it and the percipient affected by that cause have in the very act one common form which, like every universal, is the same wherever it is found. That which sees is in the act of vision in a way coloured, for it receives the same one form of colour which existed and exists in the coloured object perceived. But we may go a step further. Where one thing acts upon another, both the action and its effect reside in the patient, in that which is acted upon. Previous to their interaction, if they are physical bodies, the one is merely a potential agent, the other is merely a potential patient, whatever else they may be actually. Applying this to perception, the external thing is always perceptible, *a percipiendum*, a potential *perceptum*, the sense-faculty is always potentially percipient: but in the process of perceiving the potential in both cases has been transformed into an actual. The eye, e.g., becomes a seeing eye, the whiteness whiteness perceived, and these two actualities reside in that which is passively affected, in the sense. In other words, the actuality of the sensible object is one and the same with (not merely similar to) the actuality of the perceiving subject, sense and sensible having in the act of perception one and the same essence, since the whiteness seen in the object is transferred to the visual faculty and, being an universal, a form, is one and the same, wherever it resides. Is this, we ask, a doctrine of relativity? Most certainly not. The followers of Protagoras are supposed to argue that, if the sensible quality is alone real, nothing would exist at all unless there were living beings to perceive, for without them there would be no perception. I grant, Aristotle replies, that in the absence of living beings there would be no act of perception, no affection of the percipient. But for all that, it would be impossible to get rid of things, which are potential causes of perception even when they are never perceived. For perception does not perceive itself, there is something beyond the perception; and this must be logically prior to the perception, since whatever causes motion or change must be prior to that which it moves or changes: and this is not the less true because sensible object and percipient are relative to each other. In other words, the object perceived actually exists with its own form, its own qualities, even when it is out of all relation to a

31

percipient. And similarly we may conceive a percipient out of all relation to an object, none such being actually present. It is then what it always was, a power of perceiving, a faculty of sense, mere sensitivity.

These considerations apply most emphatically and most naturally to sense regarded as a whole, a single power which resides in the body of the animal, likewise regarded as a whole. But this power of perceiving is localised and pluralised. Wherever a part of the body subserves a particular end or function, it becomes an organ or instrument, and the general power of perception, as specialised in the five senses, employs its separate sense-organs, the eye, the ear, the nostril and the organs of taste and touch. For the detailed account of the modes in which they are employed, the medium which they necessarily imply and their special objects or provinces, the reader must be referred to Book II, Chs. 7-11. Here there is space only for a few general remarks. First, the parallelism between sense as a whole and the single special sense, e.g., sight or touch, must never be overlooked. "As the sensation of a part of the body is to that part, so is sensation as a whole to the whole sentient body as such." Thus the sense of vision presides over its own special province of colour, bounded by the opposites, white, black, and embracing every intermediate shade. The sense of touching has its special province, or rather provinces, especially temperature and resistance, bounded the former by the extremes of hot and cold, the latter of hard and soft, and including all varieties of temperature and resistance intermediate between the extremes in each province. Vision resides in the eye, touch in the internal organ of touch (probably the heart) or in the intra-organic medium, the flesh, according as we adopt the more scientific or the popular standpoint. To perceive is to undergo a qualitative change. In order, then, to become assimilated to the object, the organ must be capable of undergoing such change in the direction of either extreme or of any of the intermediate grades between these extremes. If it could not respond to the stimulus, as modern psychologists would say, at any point in the scale of colour, of temperature or of resistance, the failure on the part of the organ would be attended by mal-perception or non-perception on the part of the faculty. This is brought home to us whenever we try to employ our senses upon objects either altogether out of their range or such that the perception is attended by pernicious effects, when we try to see in the dark or to look at the noonday sun or to plunge the hand in boiling warer or to touch the air . Now what is it which justifies our expectation that in normal cases a sensible object, when present, will be perceived? What are the physical or physiological grounds on which, with the science of his day, Aristotle based this belief? He accepted from Empedocles the false physics which resolved all bodies into four elements, air, earth, fire, water, with four primary qualities, hot, cold, wet, dry. These elements are found in their compounds in the outside world. They are also found all four mixed (we might say, chemically combined) in the tissues or homogeneous parts of animal bodies, of which, again, the heterogeneous parts or organs of animal bodies are composed. Hence there is a new application of the old maxim that like is known by like. The characteristic of each object perceived depends not so much upon the materials which enter into its composition as upon the combining ratio of those materials, which constitutes its form. When Empedocles resolved bone into definite proportions of his four elements, he was not far from realising that this combining ratio is the form which makes bone what it is. So, too, with the sense-organ. It also has its combining ratio which constitutes its form, and this form, again, is the faculty residing in the organ. Hence sense as a whole, and each special sense, is a form, because it is the determining proportion or combining ratio of the tissues composing the organ. In perceiving, form receives and apprehends form. In order that it may perceive all the qualities which come within its range, the sense must be neutral or indifferent to all, must be a mean between the opposite extremes which it can perceive and be actually neither of them. In the organ of sense the constituent elements are blended in a certain way, e.g., the finger has a certain temperature. But, as by the definition perceiving is qualitative change, this temperature must be capable of variation in the direction of either extreme or of any grade intermediate to the extremes, and the constituent elements of the organ of sense must be blended in such a way as to allow of this. This possibility of variation serves to explain the discriminating power which attaches both to sense as a whole and to the single special senses. Whatever is intermediate be-tween two extremes is differently related to the one and to the other. In Aristotelian language, any point in the middle of a line is the beginning of the line in relation to one extremity, the end of the line in relation to the other. The single sense sight discriminates two shades of colour. It is in a certain relation to the first when it perceives the first, it is in a different relation to the second when it perceives the second. The discrimination measures the difference between these two relations.

The parallel between sense as a whole and the separate special senses extends to the objects directly perceived. The objects which the special senses directly perceive are known by two marks: they cannot be perceived by another special sense and the appropriate special sense cannot be mistaken about them. The objects not exclusively belonging to this or that special sense, but perceived by two or more special senses, are referred to sense as a whole, often called *sensus communis*. Such percepts are shape and magnitude, unity and number, motion, rest and time. They include what Democritus considered and Locke called the primary qualities of body. About this common function of sense as a whole there has been much needless mystification. The sentient soul is one, and all the more important and more intellectual of its functions belong to it in virtue of this unity.

As one, it perceives the common sensibles; as one, it pronounces judgments of identity and difference between sensibles; as a single faculty attendant upon each and every special sense, it is self-conscious. That to sense as a whole, the so-called *sensus communis*, should be assigned functions which in degree, if not in kind, exceed those of the separate special senses, need not surprise us. For in sense we have a whole which is something more than the sum of its different parts. Analysis into its elements does not completely explain it, nor will the simple addition of these elements reproduce what was subjected to analysis. The operation of this single faculty is temporarily arrested in sleep, permanently in death. Lastly, to this faculty belong imagination, dreams and memory, which we are now to discuss.

Sensation is defined as the production of an effect in the sense-organ, a part of the body, by an external object. It is, then, a movement or impression affecting the body and, so far as we are conscious of it, the sensitive soul as well. Now this movement does not always vanish with the disappearance of the object which caused it. Instances may be given of its persistence, as our inability at first to see in a darkened room if we have just left the sunlight; or what is known as the after-image (more correctly, the after-percept) when, if we close our eyes after looking at the sun, we see a succession of images of it in different colours. It is by facts like these that Aristotle explains imagination. He defines it as a motion generated by actual perception, a motion distinct from, yet similar to, the motion which constituted the original sensation, or, as Hobbes translates, "All fancies are motions within us, reliques of those made in the sense". In order to learn how wide is the range of the imaginative faculty we must turn to the tracts on *Sleep* and *Memory*. Sense itself is often mistaken in regard to the common sensibles and the things to which sensible qualities belong, for example, as to what the coloured or sonorous body is and where it is: and these errors of sense are shared in and increased by imagination, especially when the .sensible object is perceived from a distance. Illusion in general is due to the difference between imagination and judgment and between the standards they employ. It may sometimes be corrected by one sense coming to the aid of another, as when the object perceived as double by crossed fingers is seen to be single. The illusion that objects seem to move past us, when we in fact are travelling past them, implies that a movement is set up in the eye of the same kind as would occur if we were stationary and the objects themselves were in motion. In fact, the bodily movement induces a picture of the very object which might have been its cause. It is to the imaginative faculty that dreams must be ascribed. Sleep is the arrest of the sensitive faculty as a whole or *sensus communis,* by which when awake we are conscious that we are awake and have sensations. Plants, having no sensation, do not sleep. In order that sense, which is charged with motive as well as perceptive functions, may recover from fatigue, sleep is necessary, and it is brought about ultimately by the process of nutrition. An evaporation from the food in the stomach rises to the head, is there cooled and descends, causing a feeling of drowsiness. The surface of the body is cooled and what heat there is in the system collects about the heart. It is clear that dreaming is not a function proper to sense as a whole nor to any special sense, much less to understanding or opinion. Yet the images seen in dreams have sensible qualities. It only remains to refer dreaming to the same faculty as illusions in our waking hours. The residual movements in the organs are no doubt present in the daytime, but at night, when the action of the special senses is suspended and the environment is peaceful, the imagination is most active. Then *ex hypothesi* these persistent effects reach and stimulate the central organ of sense. We are most liable to illusions when labouring under emotion or morbid states, as, for example, when a patient in sickness mistakes figures on the wall for real animals and even makes bodily movements to escape from them. In sleep, again, the judging faculty is weak, owing to the increasing pressure of blood around the heart. There are, of course, cases in which dreams are the result of semi-conscious sensations, half-heard sounds or half-seen lights, which would have escaped attention in our waking hours: and reflections anil ideas are often added to them. But in itself dreaming is simply the result of the movement of our sensations during the period of sleep as such. Dreams are movements which give rise to images within our sense-organs.

The most important of all our images are those of memory. If imagining is consciously referred to an earlier perception of which the image is a copy, then we call it memory. For memory there are two conditions, the affection now present, and the perception of time; in other words, not only images, but images regarded as decayed copies of earlier impressions, and this involves the perception of time. By memory we see distance, not indeed in space, but in time. As memory is not confined to man, but extends to some of the lower animals, these latter must be credited with the imaginative faculty and the perception of time. Here are very promising beginnings of a comparative psychology, which Aristotle, though he desiderated it in his predecessors, did very little himself to supply. His denial of understanding to brutes was a prejudice which a little researeh would have been able to surmount. As a matter of fact, he not only holds absolutely that, though the lower animals remember, they have no reasoning power, but, further, that, if memory were a function of pure intelligence alone, even man himself could not remember, since intellectual acts cannot be remembered *per se*. What, then, can be remembered? The instrument of memory is the image. Hence whatever can be presented as an image can be directly remembered, all that cannot be presented as an image can only be remembered indirectly by means of the images with which it is associated. But how can we know the past which is not present, if our only instrument is a present affection, the image which survives after the original impression is gone? Let us revert to the formation of images. The fact that a present movement of sensation sets up a subsidiary movement of imagination may be expressed in a different way, if we employ the metaphor of an impression, by which perception has been so often illustrated. The act of perceiving, as it were, stamps a particular impression upon the sense-organ, as a seal ring stamps an impression upon wax. This impression, which remains, is a potential image so long as it is latent, an actual image when we become conscious that it is still present. Is it, then, this image, the reproduced impression, and not that of which it is an image, which we remember? If so, it may be urged, remembrance is not of the past at all. At that rate we might just as well suppose that in actual sensation also we see and hear what is not present to sense; an objection which cuts at the very root of every representative theory of perception. The objection is met by pointing out that in a certain way it is true that actual perception has for its object what is not present. We see a likeness of an absent person: the picture is present, the original is not. The picture, though numerically one and the same, may be regarded in two ways, either as a simple picture or, in relation to the original, as a likeness. Apply this to the memory-image. It, too, may be regarded in itself simply as an image before the mind, or in relation to something else of which it is a representation. If viewed in the latter aspect, it is a memorial or reminder of an earlier perception which it recalls. It is distinguished from other images by its reference to time past and by the fact that it is, what many images are not, a copy or representation. Memory may accordingly be defined not simply as a retention, but rather as a reference, of a mental presentation as a likeness to the original of which it is a likeness. All representations are likewise presentations. Images are before us in memory, in present sensation and in expectation, whether hope, fear, or desire, but we refer these images to the past, the present, and the future respectively. In all three cases something is presented, and the only way of distinguishing them is the accompanying perception of time, one of the common sensibles. Confusion of memory with imagination is one case of hallucination: thus Antipheron of Oreus was a type of mental derangement when he mistook what he only fancied for a past experience. So far, then, like imagining in general, memory is a function of *sensus communis*, and hence it is to the central organ of sense that we must refer this movement or impression or image, or whatever else we call the corporeal change in question.

The distinction between memory and reminiscence or recollection is never very clearly stated by Aristotle, but, if we attend to what he says about acquiring knowledge and reacquiring it, i.e., about learning for the first time and learning over again what we have forgotten (neither of which, of course, is to be identified with memory or recollection), it seems that the case may be put as follows. When we retain what we learn, whether by sense or thought, we are said to remember. Recollection implies the recovery of what has temporarily been obscured without going through the process of re-learning, and this whether the recovery is due to voluntary effort or is involuntary. We can remember without recollecting, if the image has never been lost, but is latent or potentially existent in us. When we recollect by voluntary effort we are conscious that it is lost and seek to recover it. Here I cite at length the account given by Wallace, p. xcv:

"Recollection may take place either intentionally or unintentionally: we may, that is to say, recall some event of past experience either accidentally as it were or by the help of a distinct effort to call it back to mind; but in either case it is regulated by certain laws which it is one of the great psychological merits of Aristotle to have tabulated for us. The laws which thus express the mode in which the mind attempts to recall its past impressions are what have commonly been designated since Aristotle's day, the Laws of the Association of Ideas. But to Aristotle, it must be added, the laws in question have little or none of the significance which they have acquired in the hands of modern inquirers. To him they are simply a statement of the manner in which we seek to regain some fragments of knowledge which have for the moment got outside our consciousness. Recollection in short being the recalling of our past impressions, it follows that the success of our efforts to recall them will depend to no inconsiderable extent on the degree to which we can recall the order in which other impressions stood to that of which we are in seareh. But our impressions follow one another in memory in an order similar to that in which the actual sensations succeeded one another. Recollection thus involves a study of the laws of sequence in the order of our ideas: and Aristotle analyses the method of recalling past impressions in the following manner. 'When engaged in recollection we seek to excite some of our previous movements, until we come to that which the movement or impression of which we are in seareh was wont to follow. And hence we seek to reach this preceding impression by starting in our thought from an object present to us or something else whether it be similar, contrary or contiguous to that of which we are in seareh; recollection taking place in this manner because the movements are in one case identical, in another case coincident and in the last case partly overlap.' Similarity, contrariety and contiguity are thus to Aristotle the three principles by which for purposes of recollection our ideas and impressions have to be guided. Our sensuous movements and impressions really follow one another in an order corresponding to that of external nature. Thus, the more order and arrangement there is in the elements of our experience - the better connected our ideas are - the more easily will they be remembered. And again the greaternumber of times we have established a connection between our ideas, the greater will be the ease with which we can recall them. Habit in short becomes a second nature: and the constant conjunction of two phenomena in outer experience will lead to their being so completely connected in the mind that the one will never show itself without the other."

I have reserved to the last the highest employment of mental images in the service of the intellect. It is impossible to think without such an image before the mind. When we are contemplating the object of thought, we must have an image before us. The past experience which we remember includes not only perceptions, but thoughts, and the reference of the image to *sensus communis* compels Aristotle to declare that nothing but what is sensible is remembered directly, *per se,* and that the whole of our thoughts, notions and conceptions are remembered indirectly, *per accidens*. Our thinking is conditioned by continuity, i.e., extension, and by time. Just as in proving a geometrical proposition we are aware that the size of the figure does not affect the proof, but we nevertheless draw the figure of a determinate size, so in thinking, even though the object is not quantitative, we think of it as a quantum, and, if it is quantitative but indefinite, we nevertheless think of it as of a definite size. What affections of sense are to the sensitive faculty, such images are to the thinking soul. The total loss of a sense cuts off the man from all the knowledge available through that sense. Without the sensations in question he will not have the corresponding images, and without them he cannot have the thoughts and conceptions. Intellect itself does not think external things without the aid of sense- perception . Further, the use of images in thinking implies their use in that process of deliberation in which the mind balances the present against the future, and after due calculation decides upon a course of action. When reason is obscured by passion, images of sense themselves directly move to action, and such images control the movements of the lower animals generally.

Book III

Intellect forms the subject of Book III, Chs. 4-8. But the detailed treatment there by no means exhausts what is said about it in the treatise. It will be convenient to collect here the more important of the scattered remarks previously made on thinking, on intellect, or even on the soul, where the context suggests that Aristotle, like Plato, is using soul for that which thinks.

If to think is a species of imagining or not independent of imagining, even thinking could not exist apart from body. Anaxagoras made soul the moving cause when he said that intelligence set the universe in motion. But, whereas Democritus absolutely identified mind with soul and did not use the term mind to denote a faculty conversant with truth, Anaxagoras was less consistent. He often made mind the cause of goodness and order; elsewhere he identified it with soul, as when he attributed it to all animals, great and small, high and low. And yet, Aristotle adds, mind in the sense of intelligence is not so widely distributed as soul or vital principle. Anaxagoras took mind as his first principle and said it alone of all existing things is simple, unmixed, pure. He attributed to one and the same principle that it knows and that it causes motion. Mind, according to him, is impassive and has nothing in common with anything else.

The criticism of the Timaeus suggests that in Aristotle's opinion the mind in the universe is not a magnitude; it is one and continuous in the same sense as the process of thinking, which consists of a series of thoughts; the unity of these thoughts is a unity of succession, the unity of number, not that of a magnitude. Hence, mind not being continuous like a magnitude, there are two alternatives: either it has no parts, or it has parts and is continuous, but not like a magnitude. A magnitude is incapable of thinking; if mind can apprehend with any one of its parts, it need not revolve nor have magnitude; it has to think two kinds of objects, the one kind divisible, the other indivisible. Thinking, as we know it, has limits which determine it, viz., the end in view or the new truths that the thinker discovers. Both thinking and inference bear far more analogy to rest or pause than to motion. In thinking the thinker ought to realise happiness. Thinking is the essence of the mind. Many held that entanglement in the body was a hindrance to thought; a satisfactory theory ought to explain why the thinking soul is enclosed in the body and under what conditions of the body.

In criticising the doctrine of harmony, he asks, what part of the bodily compound combining with the rest, can we assume to be intellect? In another connexion Aristotle says that intellect would seem to be a self-existing substance which comes into play in us and is in itself imperishable, in spite of senile decay. Thought and its exercise are enfeebled when something internal is destroyed, but the intellect in itself is impassive. Memory, love and hate are not affections of the intellect, which is something more divine and is impassive. In criticising Empedocles, Aristotle remarks that it is impossible for soul, and still more impossible for intellect, to have anything superior to it and overruling it, to it belongs a natural priority and authority. It is difficult to conjecture what part of the body intellect holds together or how it can hold together any part. After soul has been defined, we are told that there is as yet no evidence to show whether intellect is, like some of the other faculties of soul, really inseparable and only logically separable, from the rest. It would seem to be a distinct species of soul and capable of separation, as the immortal from the perishable. Sensation is of particulars, knowledge of universals, which are in a manner in the soul itself. Hence it is in our power to think whenever we please. To think is not the same thing as to have sensation, though they were identified by the ancients, who believed both to be corporeal changes. Nor is thinking the same as imagination or as belief. Imagination leads to action in the lower animals because they have no intellect, and sometimes in man when intellect is obscured by passion, disease or sleep.

What conclusions can be drawn from these scattered remarks? Apparently in one passage we have a choice of alternatives: either intellect is without parts (and therefore by the presuppositions of the Aristotelian system must be immaterial and an energy), or it is something continuous, which is, however, continuous only like a number or series, by sequence, and not by coherence, like a magnitude. A bodily organ, which has parts, would alone secure the continuity of coherence; and for such an organ there is, or so Aristotle believed, no evidence. With this agrees the tentative assumption that intellect is something impassive, independent and imperishable, since its decay in the individual is an accident and not its real essence.

The account of intellect in Book III, Chs. 4-8, is condensed and imperfect and falls far short of the clearness which marks the exposition of sense-perception. Intellect is especially concerned with quiddities and universals. It employs no bodily organ, for of the functions of the nervous system Aristotle and his contemporaries had no idea. It contains a divine element, which is independent of the body and immortal. This summary tells us hardly any more than we have collected from the casual or polemical remarks in the previous part of the treatise. But Aristotle might fairly claim to have set before us his view both of (1) the difference between intellect and sense, and (2) the way in which thinking comes about: and this is all he promised at the outset.

(1) There is an analogy between sense and intellect, there is also a difference. Both furnish knowledge, both pass judgments, both are intermittent, sometimes in act, sometimes not. When in activity both have an object, the transition from the dormant power to its actual exercise does not depend upon sense alone or upon thought alone, and, when the activity is over, the alteration thus undergone leaves intellect absolutely, and sense to a great degree, unaffected. Sensitivity in the abstract is a form which knows or apprehends sensible forms. Similarly intellect is a form which knows or apprehends intelligible forms. Moreover, in both sensation and intellection alike at the moment of apprehension, there is identity between the form which apprehends and the form which is apprehended. Again, sense-perception is always true of its own appropriate object, and similarly thinking is always true in respect of quiddities. On the other hand, the external object which stimulates the sense-faculty to activity is an individual, a particular, and it is external to the percipient; whereas the universals, the forms which we think, are present in the understanding, at any rate, of the mature man. Sensation cannot dispense with a bodily organ, a part of the body appropriated to its special functions. For intellect no such organ can be discovered. Yet, when a sense-organ is wanting, the action of intellect is impeded, for all knowledge through that

sense is cut off. Moreover, excess in the sensible fatigues or destroys the organ of sense, but the activity of thinking cannot be thus impaired. Again, intellect is the higher faculty of the two and implies the lower; the lower does not imply the higher. For actual thinking the indispensable condition is the presence of a mental image, for, as we saw above, we think of nothing apart from continuity. Even when the object conceived is not itself a quantum, we nevertheless think of it as such. And we never think of objects without thinking them in time.

(2) The process of thinking an object is explained in much the same way as the process of perceiving an object by sense. In spite of the differences stated above, both, as acts of apprehending, are assimilated to the process of reciprocal action between physical bodies. Apprehension is reception of form. If the mind knows objects by receiving them, since nothing receives what it already has, it must be assumed to be at first without them; and further, so long as it remains capable of thinking, the same condition must be fulfilled for every fresh act. Hence intellect must be impassive, suffering in no way by the change from power to act and, since it thinks all things or, in other words, is capable of receiving all forms, it must in itself be devoid of any form, though at the same time it "provides room for forms". It may be called, then, a mere aptitude or capacity to think. Until it actually thinks them, it is none of its objects, but becomes each object in turn when it thinks that object. In physical action there is a transference of essence or form: in combustion the form of heat is transferred from fire actually alight to combustible fuel. When a white object is perceived, the form of whiteness is transferred from the object to the eye and, as there is but one such form, is the same in the percipient sense as in the external object. And so when we think a stone, a horse, a triangle, the form or essence in our mind, *the* object of thought, is identically one with the form or essence outside *in rerum natura*. As a contribution to the theory of knowledge, this explanation is adequate. External things affect our sense. By sense we apprehend hot and cold and whatever other sensible qualities are accidents of flesh. We think each sensible quality, generalising and abstracting the univcrsals, of which sense by itself informs us only *per accidens*. The substance in which the attributes inhere, which is said to be indirectly perceived by sense, is directly judged and known by thought.

So far intellect has been treated as one. It is possible to apply to this unity the analysis which resolves particular things. When nature generates or art produces a concrete particular, three conditions are fulfilled. There is the efficient agent transmitting form, there is the passive recipient upon which form is impressed, and there is, lastly, the result of the process, the new particular into which matter impressed by form has been made. To manufacture a brazen sphere, we need the craftsman with the design in his mind and brass to receive that design. The form of a sphere is impressed upon the brass and a new particular is made, precisely as the form of humanity is transmitted from father to son. Our knowledge and actual thinking answer to the manufactured product, they are generated in the receptive intellect by something which must be assumed in intellect itself to correspond to the efficient cause. That which on one view is the reception of essence, is on another the spontaneous transition from potence to act. This is true of sense. Sense becomes like its object, in quality identical therewith. But it is just as true to say that sense has risen from the lower stage of potence to the higher stage of act and realised itself in full activity. So, again, thinking is reception of the form or essence, but it is just as true to say that intellect has risen from the lower stage of potence to the higher stage of act and realised itself in full activity. Perception, it is true, cannot be explained without assuming interference from without. The occasion which supplies the stimulus to the transition must be something given. With thought it is different. The occasion, the stimulus, are not external, but internal. I may say, if I like, that my potential or passive intellect has been acted upon and educed into actuality: but what brought this about? A mental agent, the active intellect, has called forth this activity and produced the thought. In my individual experience the power to think precedes actual thinking, but the transition cannot be explained except by assuming the prior existence of the efficient cause which brought it about. This point once reached and the unity of intellect being resolved into agent and patient, it follows that the agent which we postulate must have the same attributes as the patient, of which we have experience. It must be separable, impassive and unmixed, because its essence is activity, as the essence of the other factor is potentiality. Could it be actually separated and exist independently, it would be eternal. But this eternity is not communicated to the other factor of intellect, or to the intellect as a whole. Is such a hypothesis necessary? Can the potential intellect be affected by external things? So far as these things have matter in them, they are objects of thought only potentially. The intelligible forms are implicit in the sensible forms, and intellect *ex hypothesi* has no special bodily organ. But so far as knowable things are pure forms, no such expedient is required. The question, then, why an active intellect is introduced, may be thus answered. It is in order to provide a cause of that transition from potence to act which takes place whenever we actually think.

The difficulty in understanding what Aristotle did or did not intend by this analysis of the intellect, or rather this distinction of the intellect which makes, from the intellect which becomes, is notorious. The scanty comments of Theophrastus develop various lines of acute criticism, which in my judgment are not incompatible with an acceptance of the doctrine. So much is clear, that Theophrastus considered intellect in both its forms, as making and becoming, to be our human intellect, which is connatural and in us from birth to death, though its origin is elsewhere. In face of the difficulties which he is at pains to develop he seems content to regard the passive intellect dependent upon the body and the human intellect which results from the union of the passive with the active as in a sense distinct, yet as in another sense one nature, in so far as the two are related to one another as matter and form are in the unitary thing. That the active intellect exists *per se* in man independent of the passive is nowhere stated or implied either by Aristotle or Theophrastus, From a casual criticism by Themistius it appears that certain of his predecessors had identified the active intellect with the premisses from which all our knowledge is derived and with the knowledge itself which we gradually acquire. Alexander of Aphrodisias, who endeavoured to preserve faithfully the teaching of Aristotle and to present it as consistent, distinguished a material intellect and an intellect *in habitu*, which the former becomes by actual thinking and reception of the intelligible form. The material intellect is the mere aptitude for thinking: this is a power or faculty of the individual human soul, the form of the body. Lastly, there is the active intellect which is not a faculty or part of the human soul, though it is in it from birth to death whenever we actually think: not only when we think it or any of the immaterial forms with which it is identical, but also when we think forms in matter, for it is only through the agency of the active intellect that actual thinking is possible. Being wholly immaterial, energy devoid of all matter and potentiality, it always is, even when it is not thought by men; it is an eternal, imperishable, self-existent substance. There can be but one such substance: it must consequently be identified with the deity, the first cause of motion in the universe, whose nature and essence is activity, the energy of thinking. In individual men it supervenes as something coming in from outside. It finds in the capacity of thinking which does belong to the human soul an instrument ready for its use, upon which it can work and produce actual thinking. As to the reason why men think not always, Alexander has no better explanation to offer than a suggestion of his teacher, that the craftsman is still a craftsman even when he has laid aside his tools. The eclectic Themistius refused to identify the active intellect with the deity outside man. He appeals to two expressions of the master (1) "that these differences must be present in the soul," (2) "this alone is immortal and eternal," which he thinks Alexander's interpretation forces out of their natural meaning. As to (1) Alexander has his own explanation to offer, according to which the active intellect, and therefore the deity, is in our mind whenever we think: but there is some force in the contention that Aristotle would never have described the deity as "alone" immortal and eternal. However, the point in which Themistius agrees with Alexander is more important than the points in which they differ. He fully admits that the active intellect is one and the same in all men, it is distributed among different individuals as light is divided into single rays. Of the other commentators, the Neo-Platonist Simplicius distorts Aristotle's account in order, as far as possible, to adapt it to his own philosophical presuppositions. According to him, the rational human soul is one immortal substance. It has three states: in the first it remains in itself; this is the active intellect. In the second it enters the body; it then knows nothing, but is the pure potentiality of thought. Intellect of the first stage acts upon intellect of the second stage, and the result is the third stage, when intellect is *in habitu* and acquires knowledge. The passive intellect is mortal, because it ceases to be passive and is absorbed in the higher or active intellect. It is not worthwhile to pursue the course of speculation further among Arabian philosophers and the schoolmen, in both of whom the theological bias is unmistakeable. Avicenna was an original thinker who exerted a great influence on his successors; but neither his distinction of universals, *ante res*, *in rebus*, *post res*, nor his doctrine that these universals are at once substantial forms in things outside us and intelligible forms to the mind which thinks them by abstraction has any direct Aristotelian authority, and when he makes both forms alike emanate from the active intellect and ultimately from God, this doctrine becomes nearly akin to that of the Neo-Platonists. Averroes and Aquinas, though both professing to interpret Aristotle, modify his doctrines to suit their own preconceptions. According to the former, neither passive intellect nor active intellect is part of the human soul as defined in the definition. In scholastic language each is *forma assistens, superveniens* and not *forma dans esse homini.* Each is immortal and each is one and the same in all men. According to Aquinas, active intellect as well as passive intellect is a faculty of the rational human soul, which was created by the will of God and is yet immortal, having the power as form to provide a vehicle for itself after it is separated from its present body. Regarded as interpretations of Aristotle's doctrine, those two conflicting views, which divided the allegiance of the later schoolmen, cannot both be right, but may both be wrong. Aristotle himself was free from the preconceptions of his two commentators; he was not a Moslem mystic nor a Christian theologian.

These successive attempts to fill in the meagre outline presented by the text of *DeAnima* proceed in two directions. Either they make the two intellects two faculties of the human soul, or they seek to identify one, if not both, of them, with an intelligence outside man, Alexander, Averroes, and in modern times, Ravaisson and Renan, have gone to the greatest lengths in the latter direction. But, if the act of thinking is independent of, or alien to, man's nature, how can the aptitude for thinking be any longer a part of it? Averroes no doubt is consistent: he declares the passive intellect also to be an immaterial substance and no part of the soul which is the form of the human body. But, in order to maintain this, he is obliged to do violence to the language of the treatise. In particular, his *virtus cogitativa*, with which, according to him, the definition of soul endows man, has to be divorced from intellect proper and reduced nearly to the level of *sensus communis* or imagination. Even then he is unable to explain why, after the definition of soul has been obtained, it should have been left an open question whether intellect properly so called is or is not a part of the soul, or why it should be designated as a "part" when at last it comes up for special treatment. But in fact all views in which human intellect or a part of it is identified with the activity of divine intellect are met by the same insoluble difficulty: what is to be made of the intellect which becomes all things? Modern enquirers are hopelessly divided as to what the passive intellect is. Trendelenburg answers "all the lower faculties in contradistinction to the active intellect", Zeller "the sum of those faculties of representation which go beyond imagination and sensible perception and yet fall short of that higher Thought, which has found peace in perfect unity with its object", Ravaisson " the universal potentiality in the world of ideas", Brentano "imagination", Hertling "the cognitive faculty of the sensitive part", and Hammond, if I understand him rightly, "the life of sensation as a potentially rational mass", "the sum of the deliverances of sense-perception and their re-wrought form in memory and phantasy, regarded as potentiality". The last two would seem almost to identify its functions with those of *sensus communis* as a judging faculty. Now these various answers do not accord with the description in *De Anima* of the process and act of thinking, whether as apprehension of the intelligible object or as the judgment which makes two concepts one; they do not fit either the conception of intellect *in habitu*, the process by which knowledge is acquired, or the sharp distinction drawn between a thought and a mental image. Thinking is not the same as receiving or retaining or remembering or judging the percepts of sense, which are all individual and lack the universality required. Abstraction alone renders thought possible, and abstraction cannot be restricted to the active intellect. Again, all the operations of thought imply a single judging power. This position, which Aristotle has maintained for sense, he would certainly maintain as strongly for thought. When he controverts the Protagorean maxim and points out that it must lead to universal relativity, he contends that there is such a thing as absolute existence, a something determinate in itself apart from all relations, for presentation of an object implies a subject to whom the object is presented. The object of thought, then, implies a thinking subject. If these modern interpreters were right in equating the intellect which becomes with one or other of the lower faculties or with the sum of them, then the functions of these faculties would be identical with the function of thought, so far as the intellect becomes all things. But the lower faculties, sense and imagination, never succeed in obtaining an object which is a true universal.

If, however, we vindicate the right to think for the intellect which becomes all objects and is said to be *in habitu* it when it acquires knowledge, it would seem that this can only be clone at the expense of the intellect which makes all objects. The functions of the latter are then reduced within the narrowest compass. According to some, it does not really think at all, it docs little more than "illuminate" the mental image, thus facilitating the abstraction of the universal form. But Aristotle speaks of its perpetual activity, he says there is no intermission in its thought. Yet it is not unreasonable to suppose that determinations so unlike as "pure potentiality" and "incessant activity" refer to the same thing under two different aspects. Each describes it abstractly, and, to know the whole, the two determinations must be combined. If there is within us a thought which is continuous and always in activity, at any rate experience does not tell us so, it can only be a conclusion of reason. How, then, did Aristotle reconcile this conclusion with the facts? Apparently he made this thinking latent. The intellect always thinks, but we do not remember. This, then, is what the attribute "potential" means as applied to the intellect; and this agrees with the conception of the powers or faculties of the soul in general, which are permanent possessions, all dormant and unconscious, until roused to activity in consciousness. Here we may recall a previous use of the antithesis between potential and actual in Aristotle's account of hnaginatinn. The images or survivals of sensation are not always present to consciousness, yet Aristotle treats them as still in existence; they continue, he says, in the organs of sense, they are potential images while they are dormant, actual images when they are revived and reappear, as we should say, in consciousness. It may be worthwhile to hazard the conjecture that the intellect which does not consciously think is similarly described as potential intellect, and yet all the time its thoughts are there, though its incessant activity is subconscious. It will be seen that, though I do not entirely agree with Wallace, I nevertheless recognise a certain element of truth in his solution of the difficulty. He thus conceives the relation of the two intellects: "the creative reason is the faculty which constantly interprets and as it were keeps up an intelligible world for experience to operate upon, while the receptive reason is the intellect applying itself in all the various processes which fill our minds with the materials of knowledge". And again: "the two it must be remembered are not 'two reasons': they are merely different m*odes* of viewing the work of reason".

In the account of sense and thought, with which we have been hitherto mainly occupied, the cognitive element is very prominent. It is natural to infer that our philosopher regards man chiefly on the intellectual side, as a spectator of the universe, a being who contemplates. And this impression would seem to be confirmed when we learn from the *Ethics* wherein man's chief good consists. But no Greek could overlook the other side of human nature. The conclusions of the *Ethics* must be taken in conjunction with the wider generalisations of the *Politics*; and, if the self or ego is identical with intellect, intellect is practical as well as theoretic. The true is in the same class with the good; good, real or apparent, is the goal of all striving and effort. With his teleological bias, Aristotle would have endorsed the words of a modern psychologist: "Looking broadly at the progress of life, as it ascends through the animal kingdom and onwards through the history of man, it seems safe to say that knowledge is always a means to ends, is never an end by itself - till at length it becomes interesting and satisfying in itself. Psychologically, then, the sole function of perception and intellection is to guide action and subserve volition - more generally, to promote self-conservation and betterment." In *De Anima*, a professedly biological treatise, with the soul in all living things for its subject, this part of the enquiry is not pushed far. The main outlines are given, but we must look elsewhere, and particularly to the *Ethics*, for further details. The problem is presented in a very simple fashion. In the animal world motion, in the sense of locomotion is an all-pervading fact, and but slight observation suffices to show that this motion is not random or irregular, but is directed to an end. To what power or faculty, then, is it to be ascribed? The nutritive faculty, Aristotle thinks, sufficiently accounts for movements of growth and decay, whether in animals or plants, but not for the progressive movements of animals, movements prompted by want and directed to an end. If the nutritive faculty were sufficient to produce such movements, Aristotle adds with unconscious irony, plants would move spontaneously and would have organs adapted for the purpose. Nor can these movements be explained as due to the sensitive faculty, since there are whole genera of perfectly-developed animals of a low type which do not move from place to place. But if locomotion were implied in sensation, they, too, would have organs adapted for locomotion. Is intellect, then, the cause of which we are in seareh, as Plato thought? No. Intellect is either theoretical or practical. The former issues no command as to what we should avoid or pursue and, although the latter does issue such commands, they are not necessarily obeyed. The analogy of the arts, too, shows that, in order to produce action, something else is required beyond the mere knowledge of what is to be pursued or avoided. Shall we say, then, that there are two motives to action, (1) desire and (2) the intellect which calculates means to ends, the place of which latter in animals devoid of reason is taken by imagination? If so, how are the two connected? Desire is always of an end, and this end is the starting point for the calculations of the practical intellect. Intellect and desire, then, are connected by the ultimate unmoved movement, the end of action. It is this which stirs desire, while intellect, assuming that the end can be realised, calculates the steps towards its attainment. Thus the physician whose aim is to cure an ague assumes this to be done, just as if he were trying to solve a geometrical problem, and then reasons backwards from the patient's recovery to the normal temperature which this implies, from the normal temperature to the production of heat or cold, and from that to some remedy at his command;and thereupon, having reached the end of his calculations, he proceeds to act. Hence the statement that there are two motives to action calls for qualification. Had there been two, they would have had some common character, but as a matter of fact intellect is never a motive apart from desire. On the other hand, desire does sometimes move to action in spite of reason. Desire is thus found in all forms of mental life. In reason it is rational wish, but there are also irrational desires, anger and appetite, or mere desire of pleasure. In fact, an appetitive faculty must be assumed in which Plato's anger and appetite are both included, and Aristotle says quite fairly that the soul may be divided into many faculties, any two of which are more distinct than these two of Plato. Wherever in the animal world there is sense-perception, there is also the feeling of pleasure and pain. The pleasurable prompts desire, the painful aversion, and the survival of sense-impressions, which is imagination in its lowest form, can prompt to desire no less than the present object in the moment of perception. For the intellect images take the place of present sensation. A conflict of desires may arise, for though reason will judge correctly, anger or appetite may be blinded. They may take apparent good for real good, or they may interpret good as the pleasure of the moment. Every desire, whether rational or irrational, implies a corresponding image of the object desired. Hence a distinction between images, according as they proceed wholly from sense (and this class of images alone belongs to irrational animals) or proceed from reason, calculation; in fact, deliberation. This latter class of images is peculiar to man. Yet even in man in the abnormal state of incontinence the irrational desire gets the better of reason and controls action. In order to ex- press the antecedents of action, whether of the normal or abnormal kind, Aristotle resorted to the analogy of the syllogism. From a universal major premiss and a particular minor a conclusion is inferred. For example, all men should take exercise, Callias is a man, *ergo* Callias should take exercise. His taking exercise is regarded as an inference from the premisses. It resembles the conclusion of a syllogism just in so far as a particular case is brought under a general rule. But this way of looking at the matter by no means ensures rational action or justifies the assumption that the intellect always calculates correctly, for incontinence has a syllogism of its own. For example, all sweet things are to be tasted, this thing before me is sweet: then, if you have the power and are not hindered, you cannot but at once put the conclusion (this is to be tasted) into practice. In this way the triumph of the irrational impulse and the sacrifice of the permanent good to the pleasure of the moment may equally be considered to bring a particular case under a general rule. In other words, although reason has a natural right and ought to prevail, experience shows that it is not always effective, even in beings endowed with reason, who look before and after. When impulsive action has been distinguished from deliberative and we are dealing with the latter only, since purpose is desire following upon deliberation, if the purpose is to be all it should be, both the calculation or reasoning must be true and the desire right, and the very same things must be assented to by the reason and pursued by the desire.

In the foregoing sketch I have been content to let Aristotle speak for himself, piecing together various utterances and putting the best construction I could on what is obscure and enigmatical in them, but refraining as a rule from criticism. Obviously he studied psychology as a philosopher and was chiefly interested in it as it bore upon philosophical problems. He exalted the cognitive element, while his treatment of the emotions and the will is wholly inadequate, even if the *Ethics* and the *Rhetoric* be called in to redress the balance. It is now contended that the science of psychology, which has made vast strides since these humble beginnings, must be based exclusively upon individual experience and be made independent of physiology. Whatever can be set down to the credit of Aristotle as a psychologist rests upon the opposite assumptions. He approached his subject from the psychophysical standpoint, as it is called; he had his own representative theory of perception, his own account of the gradual ascent from sense, through memory, to science and reason. He coulcl not escape the errors and confusion incident to such assumptions, if after all they are not ultimately valid. Thus we are brought face to face with grave metaphysical problems. But this is not the place to examine Aristotle's system as a whole, and without such an examination it is impossible to do justice either to his theory of knowledge or to the treatise on the soul.

R. D. Hicks
Cambridge University, 1907

BOOK I

Chapter 1

Cognition is in our eyes a thing of beauty and worth, and this is true of one cognition more than another, either because it is exact or because it relates to more important and remarkable objects. On both these grounds we may with good reason claim a high place for the enquiry concerning the soul. It would seem, too, that an acquaintance with the subject contributes greatly to the whole domain of truth and, more particularly, to the study of nature, the soul being virtually the principle of all animal life.

Our aim is to discover and ascertain the nature and essence of soul and, in the next place, all the accidents belonging to it; of which some are thought to be attributes peculiar to the soul itself, while others, it is held, belong to the animal also, but owe their existence to the soul. But everywhere and in every way it is extremely difficult to arrive at any trustworthy conclusion on the subject. It is the same here as in many other enquiries. What we have to investigate is the essential nature of things and the What. It might therefore be thought that there is a single procedure applicable to all the objects whose essential nature we wish to discover, as demonstration is applicable to the properties which go along with them: in that case we should have to enquire what this procedure is. If, however, there is no single procedure common to all sciences for defining the What, our task becomes still more difficult, as it will then be necessary to settle in each particular case the method to be pursued. Further, even if it be evident that it consists in demonstration of some sort or division or some other procedure, there is still room for much perplexity and error, when we ask from what premisses our enquiry should start, for there are different premises for different sciences; for the science of numbers, for example, and plane geometry.

The first thing necessary is no doubt to determine under which of the summa genera soul comes and what it is; I mean, whether it is a particular thing, i.e. substance, or is quality or is quantity, or falls under any other of the categories already determined. We must further ask whether it is amongst things potentially existent or is rather a sort of actuality, the distinction being all-important. Again, we must consider whether it is divisible or indivisible; whether, again, all and every soul is homogeneous or not; and, if not, whether the difference between the various souls is a difference of species or a difference of genus: for at present discussions and investigations about soul would appear to be restricted to the human soul. We must take care not to overlook the question whether there is a single definition of soul answering to a single definition of animal; or whether there is a different definition for each separate soul, as for horse and dog, man and god: animal, as the universal, being regarded either as non-existent or, if existent, as logically posterior. This is a question which might equally be raised in regard to any other common predicate. Further, on the assumption that there are not several souls, but merely several different parts in the same soul, it is a question whether we should begin by investigating soul as a whole or its several parts. And here again it is difficult to determine which of these parts are really distinct from one another and whether the several parts, or their functions, should be investigated first. Thus, e.g., should the process of thinking come first or the mind that thinks, the process of sensation or the sensitive faculty? And so everywhere else. But, if the functions should come first, again will arise the question whether we should first investigate the correlative objects. Shall we take, e.g., the sensible object before the faculty of sense and the intelligible object before the intellect?

It would seem that not only is the knowledge of a thing's essential nature useful for discovering the causes of its attributes, as, e.g., in mathematics the knowledge of what is meant by the terms straight or curved, line or surface, aids us in discovering to how many right angles the angles of a triangle are equal: but also, conversely, a knowledge of the attributes is a considerable aid to the knowledge of what a thing is. For when we are able to give an account of all, or at any rate most, of the attributes as they are presented to us, then we shall be in a position to define most exactly the essential nature of the thing. In fact, the starting point of every demonstration is a definition of what something is. Hence the definitions which lead to no information about attributes and do not facilitate even conjecture respecting them have clearly been framed for dialectic and are void of content, one and all.

A further difficulty arises as to whether all attributes of the soul are also shared by that which contains the soul or whether any of them are peculiar to the soul itself: a question which it is indispensable, and yet by no means easy, to decide. It would appear that in most cases soul neither acts nor is acted upon apart from the body: as, e.g., in anger, confidence, desire and sensation in general. Thought, if anything, would seem to be peculiar to the soul. Yet, if thought is a sort of imagination, or not independent of imagination, it will follow that even thought cannot be independent of the body. If, then, there be any of the functions or affections of the soul peculiar to it, it will be possible for the soul to be separated from the body: if, on the other hand, there is nothing of the sort peculiar to it, the soul will not be capable of separate existence. As with the straight line, so with it. The line, *quâ* straight, has many properties; for instance, it touches the brazen sphere at a point; but it by no means follows that it will so touch it if separated. In fact it is inseparable, since it is always conjoined with body of some sort. So, too, the attributes of the soul appear to be all conjoined with body: such attributes, viz., as anger, mildness, fear, pity, courage; also joy, love and hate; all of which are attended by some particular affection of the body. This indeed is shown by the fact that sometimes violent and palpable incentives occur without producing in us exasperation or fear, while at other times we are moved by slight and scarcely perceptible causes, when the blood is up and the bodily condition that of anger. Still more is this evident from the fact that sometimes even without the occurrence of anything terrible men exhibit all the symptoms of terror. If this be so, the attributes are evidently forms or notions realised in matter. Hence they must be defined accordingly: anger, for instance, as a certain movement in a body of a given kind, or some part or faculty of it, produced by such and such a cause and for such and such an end. These facts at once bring the investigation of soul, whether in its entirety or in the particular aspect described, within the province of the natural philosopher. But every such attribute would be differently defined by the physicist and the dialectician or philosopher. Anger, for instance, would be defined by the dialectician as desire for retaliation or the like, by the physicist as a ferment of the blood or heat which is about the heart: the one of them gives the matter, the other the form or notion. For the notion is the form of the thing, but this notion, if it is to be, must be realised in matter of a particular kind; just as in the case of a house. The notion or definition of a house would be as follows: a shelter to protect us from harm by wind or rain or scorching heat; while another will describe it as stones, bricks and timber; and again another as the form realised in these materials and subserving given ends. Which then of these is the true physicist? Is it he who confines himself to the matter, while ignoring the form? Or he who treats of the form exclusively? I answer, it is rather he who in his definition takes account of both. What then of each of the other two? Or shall we rather say that there is no one who deals with properties which are not separable nor yet treated as separable, but the physicist deals with all the active properties or passive affections belonging to body of a given sort and the corresponding matter? All attributes not regarded as so belonging he leaves to someone else: who in certain cases is an expert, a carpenter, for instance, or a physician. The attributes which, though in separable, are not regarded as properties of body of a given sort, but are reached by abstraction, fall within the province of the mathematician: while attributes which are regarded as having separate existence fall to the first philosopher or metaphysician. But to return to the point of digression. We were saying that the attributes of the soul are as such, I mean, as anger and fear inseparable from the physical matter of the animals to which they belong, and not, like line and surface, separable in thought.

Chapter 2

In our enquiry concerning soul it is necessary to state the problems which must be solved as we proceed, and at the same time to collect the views of our predecessors who had anything to say on the subject, in order that we may adopt what is right in their conclusions and guard against their mistakes. Our enquiry will begin by presenting what are commonly held to be in a special degree the natural attributes of soul. Now there are two points especially wherein that which is animate is held to differ from the inanimate, namely, motion and the act of sensation: and these are approximately the two characteristics of soul handed down to us by our predecessors. There are some who maintain that soul is preeminently and primarily the cause of movement. But they imagined that that which is not itself in motion cannot move anything else, and thus they regarded the soul as a thing which is in motion. Hence Democritus affirms the soul to be a sort of fire or heat. For the "shapes" or atoms are infinite and those which are spherical he declares to be fire and soul: they may be compared with the so-called motes in the air, which are seen in the sunbeams that enter through our windows. The aggregate of such seeds, he tells us, forms the constituent elements of the whole of nature (and herein he agrees with Leucippus), while those of them which are spherical form the soul, because such figures most easily find their way through everything and, being themselves in motion, set other things in motion. The atomists assume that it is the soul which imparts motion to animals. It is for this reason that they make life depend upon respiration. For, when the surrounding air presses upon bodies and tends to extrude those atomic shapes which, because they are never at rest themselves, impart motion to animals, then they are reinforced from outside by the entry of other like atoms in respiration, which in fact, by helping to check compression and solidification, prevent the escape of the atoms already contained in the animals; and life, so they hold, continues so long as there is strength to do this. The doctrine of the Pythagoreans seems also to contain the, same thought. Some of them identified soul with the motes in the air, others with that which sets these motes in motion: and as to these motes it has been stated that they are seen to be in incessant motion, even though there be a perfect calm. The view of others who describe the soul as that which moves itself tends in the same direction. For it would seem that all these thinkers regard motion as the most distinctive characteristic of the soul. Everything else, they think, is moved by the soul, but the soul is moved by itself: and this because they never see anything cause motion without itself being in motion. Similarly the soul is said to be the moving principle by Anaxagoras and all others who have held that mind sets the universe in motion; but not altogether in the same sense as by Democritus. The latter, indeed, absolutely identified soul and mind, holding that the presentation to the senses is the truth: hence, he observed, Homer had well sung of Hector in his swoon that he lay 'with other thoughts'. Democritus, then, does not use the term mind to denote a faculty conversant with truth, but regards mind as identical with soul. Anaxagoras, however, is less exact in his use of the terms. In many places he speaks of mind as the cause of goodness and order, but elsewhere he identifies it with the soul: as where he attributes it to all animals, both great and small, high and low. As a matter of fact, however, mind in the sense of intelligence would not seem to be present in all animals alike, nor even in all men.

Those, then, who have directed their attention to the motion of the animate being, conceived the soul as that which is most capable of causing motion: while those who laid stress on its knowledge and perception of all that exists identified the soul with the ultimate principles, whether they recognised a plurality of these or only one. Thus Empedocles compounded soul out of all the elements, while at the same time regarding each one of them as a soul. His words are "With earth we see earth, with water water, with air bright air, but ravaging fire by fire, love by love, and strife by gruesome strife". In the same manner Plato in the *Timaeus* constructs the soul out of the elements. Like, he there maintains, is known by like, and the things we know are composed of the ultimate principles. In like manner it was explained in the lectures on philosophy, that the self-animal or universe is made up of the idea of One, and of the idea-numbers Two, or primary length, Three, primary breadth, and Four, primary depth, and similarly with all the rest of the ideas. And again this has been put in another way as follows: reason is the One, knowledge is the Two, because it proceeds by a single road to one conclusion, opinion is the number of a surface, Three, and sensation the number of a solid, Four. In fact, according to them the numbers, though they are the ideas themselves, or the ultimate principles, are nevertheless derived from elements. And things are judged, some by reason, others by knowledge, others again by opinion and others by sensation: while these idea-numbers are forms of things. And since the soul was held to be thus cognitive as well as capable of causing motion, some thinkers have combined the two and defined the soul as a self-moving number.

But there are differences of opinion as to the nature and number of various the ultimate principles, especially between those thinkers theories of who make the principles corporeal and those who make them incorporeal; and again between both of these and others who combine the two and take their principles from both. But, further, they differ also as to their number: some assuming a single principle, some a plurality. And, when they come to give an account of the soul, they do so in strict accordance with their several views. For they have assumed, not unnaturally, that the soul is that primary cause which in its own nature is capable of producing motion. And this is why some identified soul with fire, this being the element which is made up of the finest particles and is most nearly incorporeal, while further it is preeminently an element which both moves and sets other things in motion. Democritus has expressed more neatly the reason for each of these facts. Soul he regards as identical with mind, and this he makes to consist of the primary indivisible bodies and considers it to be a cause of motion from the fineness of its particles and their shape. Now the shape which is most susceptible of motion is the spherical; and of atoms of this shape mind, like fire, consists. Anaxagoras, while apparently understanding by mind something different from soul, as we remarked above, really treats both as a single nature, except that it is preeminently mind which he takes as his first principle; he says at any rate that mind alone of things that exist is simple, unmixed, pure. But he refers both knowledge and motion to the same principle, when he says that mind sets the universe in motion. Thales, too, apparently, judging from the anecdotes related of him, conceived soul as a cause of motion, if it be true that he affirmed the loadstone to possess soul, because it attracts iron. Diogenes, however, as also some others, identified soul with air. Air, they thought, is made up of the finest particles and is the first principle: and this explains the fact that the soul knows and is a cause of motion, knowing by virtue of being the primary element from which all else is derived, and causing motion by the extreme fineness of its parts. Heraclitus takes soul for his first principle, as he identifies it with the vapour from which he derives all other things, and further says that it is the least corporeal of things and in ceaseless flux; and that it is by something in motion that what is in motion is known; for he, like most philosophers, conceived all that exists to be in motion. Alcmaeon, too, seems to have had a similar conception. For soul, he maintains, is immortal because it is like the beings which are immortal; and it has this attribute in virtue of being ever in motion: for he attributes continuous and unending motion to everything which is divine, moon, sun, stars and the whole heaven. Among cruder thinkers there have been some, like Hippon, who have even asserted the soul to be water. The reason for this view seems to have been the fact that in all animals the seed is moist: in fact, Hippon refutes those who make the soul to be blood by pointing out that the seed is not blood, and that this seed is the rudimentary soul. Others, again, like Critias, maintain the soul to be blood, holding that it is sentience which is most distinctive of soul and that this is due to the nature of blood. Thus each of the four elements except earth has found its supporter. Earth, however, has not been put forward by anyone, except by those who have explained the soul to be derived from, or identical with, all the elements.

Thus practically all define the soul by three characteristics, motion, perception and incorporeality; and each of these characteristics is referred to the ultimate principles. Hence all who define soul by its capacity for knowledge either make it an element or derive it from the elements, being on this point, with one exception, in general agreement. Like, they tell us, is known by like; and therefore, since the soul knows all things, they say it consists of all the ultimate principles. Thus those thinkers who admit only one cause and one element, as fire or air, assume the soul also to be one element; while those who admit a plurality of principles assume plurality also in the soul. Anaxagoras alone says that mind cannot be acted upon and has nothing in common with any other thing. How, if such be its nature, it will know anything and how its knowledge is to be explained, he has omitted to state; nor do his utterances afford a clue. All those who introduce pairs of opposites among their principles make the soul also to consist of opposites; while those who take one or other of the two opposites, either hot or cold or something else of the sort, reduce the soul also to one or other of these elements. Hence, too, they etymologise according to their theories; some identify soul with heat, deriving ζῆν from ζεῖν, and contend that this identity accounts for the word for life; others say that what is cold is called soul from the respiratory process and consequent "cooling down", deriving ψυχή from ψύχειν. Such, then, are the views regarding soul which have come down to us and the grounds on which they are held.

Chapter 3

We have to consider in the first place the subject of motion. For, unless I am mistaken, the definition of soul as the self-moving, or as that which is capable of self-motion, misrepresents its essential nature: nay, more; it is quite impossible for soul to have the attribute of motion at all. To begin with, it has been already stated that a thing may cause motion without necessarily being moved itself. A thing is always moved in one of two ways; that is, either indirectly, through something else, or directly, of and through itself. We say things are moved through something else when they are in something else that is moved: as, for instance, sailors on board a ship: for they do not move in the same sense as the ship, for the ship moves of itself, they because they are in something else which is moved. This is evident if we consider the members of the body: for the motion proper to the feet and so to men also is walking, but it is not attributable to our sailors in the case supposed. There being thus two senses in which the term "to be moved" is used, we are now enquiring whether it is of and through itself that the soul is moved and partakes of motion.

Of motion there are four species, change of place or locomotion, change of quality or alteration, diminution and augmentation. It is, then, with one or more or all of these motion. species that the soul will move. If it is not indirectly or *per accidens* that it moves, motion will be a natural attribute of soul; and, if this be so, it will also have position in space, since all the aforesaid species of motion are in space. But, if it be the essential nature of soul to move itself, motion will not be an accidental attribute of soul, as it is of whiteness or the length of three cubits; for these are also moved, but *per accidens*, viz. by the motion of the body to which these attributes belong. This, too, is why these attributes have no place belonging to them; but the soul will have a place, if indeed motion is its natural attribute.

Further, if it moves naturally, then it will also move under constraint; and, if under constraint, then also naturally. So likewise with rest. For, as it remains at rest naturally in any state into which it moves naturally, so similarly it remains at rest by constraint in any state into which it moves by constraint. But what is meant by constrained motions or states of rest of the soul it is not easy to explain, even though we give free play to fancy. Again, if its motion tends upward, it will be fire; if downward, earth; these being the motions proper to these natural bodies. And the same argument applies to directions of motion which are intermediate.

Again, since it appears that the soul sets the body in motion, it may reasonably be supposed to impart to it the motions which it has itself: and, if so, then conversely it is true to say that the motion which the soul has itself is the motion which the body has. Now the motion of the body is motion in space: therefore the motion of the soul is also motion in space, whether the whole soul so move, or only the parts, the whole remaining at rest. But, if this is admissible, the soul might also conceivably quit the body and re-enter; and this would involve the consequence that dead animals may rise again.

To return now to motion *per accidens*, soul might certainly thus be moved by something external as well: for the animal might be thrust by force. But a thing which has self-motion as part of its essential nature cannot be moved from without except incidentally; any more than that which is good in itself can be means to an end, or that which is good for its own sake can be so for the sake of something else. But, supposing the soul to be moved at all, one would say that sensible things would be the most likely to move it.

Again, even if soul does move itself, this is equivalent to saying that it is moved; and, all motion being defined as displacement of the thing moved *quâ* moved, it will follow that the soul will be displaced from its own essential nature, if it be true that its self-movement is not an accident, but that motion belongs to the essence of soul in and of itself. Some say that the soul in fact moves the body, in which it is, in the same way in which it moves itself. So, for example, Democritus; and herein he resembled Philippus, the comic poet, who tells us that Daedalus endowed the wooden Aphrodite with motion, simply by pouring in quicksilver: this is very similar to what Democritus says. For according to him the spherical atoms, which from their nature can never remain still, being moved, tend to draw the whole body after them and thus set it in motion. But do these same atoms, we shall ask in our turn, produce rest, as well as motion? How this should be, it is difficult, if not impossible, to say. And, speaking generally, it is not in this way that the soul would seem to move the animal, but by means of purpose of some sort, that is, thought.

In the same way the Platonic *Timaeus* explains on physical grounds that the soul sets the body in motion, for by its own motion it sets the body also in motion, because it is closely interwoven with it. For when it had been made out of the elements and divided in harmonical ratios in order that it might have a native perception of proportion and that the universe might move in harmonic revolutions, he, the creator, proceeded to bend the straight line into a circle; and then to split the one circle into two, intersecting at two points; and one of the two circles he split into seven, the revolutions of heaven being regarded as the motions of the soul. In the first place, it is not right to call the soul a magnitude. For by the soul of the universe *Timaeus* clearly intends something of the same sort as what is known as mind: he can hardly mean that it is like the sensitive or appetitive soul, whose movements are not circular. But the thinking mind is one and continuous in the same sense as the process of thinking. Now thinking consists of thoughts. But the unity of these thoughts is a unity of succession, the unity of a number, and not the unity of a magnitude. This being so, neither is mind continuous in this latter sense, but either it is without parts or else it is continuous in a different sense from an extended magnitude. For how can it possibly think if it be a magnitude? Will it think with some one or other of its parts: such parts being taken either in the sense of magnitudes or in the sense of points, if a point can be called a part? If it be with parts in the sense of points, and there is an infinity of these, clearly mind will never reach the end of them; while, if they be taken in the sense of magnitudes, mind will have the same thoughts times without end. But experience shows that we can think a thought once and no more. Again, if it be enough for the soul to apprehend with one or other of its parts, what need is there for it to be moving in a circle or to have magnitude at all? But, if it is necessary to thought that the mind should bring the whole circle into contact, what does the contact of the several parts mean? Again, how will it think that which is divisible by means of that which is without parts, or that which is without parts by means of that which is divisible? It must be mind which is meant by the circle in question. For when mind moves it thinks; when a circle moves it revolves. If, then, thought is a revolution, the circle which has such a revolution must be mind. But then it will go on thinking of something for ever, for this is required by the eternity of the revolution. To practical thinking there are limits, for it always implies an external end; while speculative thinking is determined in the same way as the logical explanations which express it. Now every explanation consists either in definition or in demonstration. But demonstrations have a premiss for starting-point and reach a kind of goal in the inference or conclusion; while, even if they never reach a conclusion, at all events they do not revert to the starting-point, but with the aid of a succession of middle terms and extremes advance in a straight line. But circular movement returns to the point from which it started. Definitions, too, are all determinate. Besides, if the same revolution recurs again and again, the mind will be obliged to think the same thing again and again. Further, it is a sort of rest or coming to a halt, and not motion, which thinking resembles: and we may say the same of the syllogism. Nor, again, will that which does not move easily, but under constraint, even realise happiness. If the motion of soul be not its essence, it will be an unnatural motion. And the entanglement of the mind in the body without the possibility of release is painful; nay, it is to be avoided, if indeed it is really better for mind to be independent of body, a view commonly expressed and widely accepted. Also it is not clear why the heaven revolves in a circle; seeing that circular motion is neither implied by the essence of soul (that form of movement being indeed merely accidental to it), nor due to the body: on the contrary it is rather the soul which causes the motion of the body. Besides, we are not even told that it is better so: yet surely the reason why God made the soul revolve in a circle ought to have been that movement was better for it than rest, and this form of movement better than any other.

But such an enquiry as this belongs more appropriately to a different subject: so let us dismiss it for the present. We may, however, note here another absurdity which is involved in this as in most other theories concerning the soul. They attach between the soul to, and enclose it in, body, without further determining

61

why this happens and what is the condition of the body. And yet some such explanation would seem to be required, as it is owing to their relationship that the one acts, the other is acted upon, that the one is moved, and the other causes it to move; and between two things taken at random no such mutual relations exist The supporters of such theories merely undertake to explain the nature of the soul. Of the body which is to receive it they have nothing more to say: just as if it were possible for any soul taken at random, according to the Pythagorean stories, to pass into any body. This is absurd, for each body appears to have a distinctive form or shape of its own. It is just like talking of a transmigration of carpentry into flutes: for the craft must employ the right tools and the soul the right body.

Chapter 4

There is yet another opinion concerning soul which has come down to us, commending itself to many minds as readily as any that is put forward, although it has been severely criticised even in the popular discussions of the present day. The soul is asserted to be a kind of harmony, for harmony is on this view a blending or combining of opposites, and the components of the body are opposites. And yet this harmony must mean either a certain proportion in the components or else the combining of them; and the soul cannot possibly be either of these. Furthermore, to cause motion is no attribute of a harmony: yet this function more than any other is all but universally assigned to soul. Again, it is more in harmony with the facts to apply the term harmony to health or bodily excellence generally than to soul, as is very clearly seen when we try to assign to a harmony of whatever kind the affections or functions of the soul: it is difficult to harmonise them.

Further, if we use the word harmony with a twofold application; first, and in its most natural sense, of those magnitudes which have motion and position, to denote the combining of them into a whole, when they are so closely fitted together that they do not admit between them anything of the same kind; and then in a secondary sense to denote the proportion subsisting between the components of a mixture: in neither sense is it reasonable to call soul a harmony. The view which regards it as a combining of the parts of the body is singularly open to criticism. For there are many combinings of the parts, and they combine in many ways. What part, then, is that whose combining with the rest we must assume to be the intellect, and in what way does it combine? Or again, what of the sensitive and appetitive faculties? But it is equally absurd to regard the soul as the proportion determining the mixture. For the elements are not mixed in the same proportion in flesh as in bone. Thus it will follow that there are many souls, and that, too, all over the body, if we assume that all members consist of the elements variously commingled and that the proportion determining the mixture is a harmony, that is, soul. This is a question we might ask Empedocles; who says that each of the parts is determined by a certain proportion. Is the soul, then, this proportion, or is it rather developed in the frame as something distinct? And, further, is it a mixture at random or a mixture in the right proportion which he ascribes to Love: and, if the latter, is Love the proportion itself or something other than the proportion and distinct from it? Such, then, are the difficulties involved in this view. On the other hand, if soul is something distinct from the mixture, how comes it that it is destroyed simultaneously with the disappearance of the quiddity of the flesh and of the other parts of the animal? And, further, assuming that each of the separate parts has not a soul of its own, unless the soul be the proportion of their admixture, what is it that perishes when the soul quits the body?

From what has been said it is clear that the soul cannot be a harmony and cannot revolve in a circle. But incidentally it can, as we have seen, move and set itself in motion: for instance, the body in which it is may move, and be set in motion by the soul: otherwise it cannot possibly move from place to place. The question whether the soul is moved would more naturally arise in view of such facts as the following. The soul is said to feel pain and joy, confidence and fear, and again to be angry, to perceive and to think; and all these states are held to be movements: which might lead one to infer that soul itself is moved. But this is no necessary inference. For suppose it ever so true that to feel pain or joy and to think are movements, that to experience each of these is to be moved and that the movement is due to the soul: suppose that to be angry, for instance, or to be afraid means a particular movement of the heart, and that to think means a movement of this or of some other part, some of these movements being movements of locomotion, others of qualitative change (of what sort and how produced does not concern us here): yet, even then, to speak of the soul as feeling anger is as if one should say that the soul weaves or builds. Doubtless it would be better not to say that the soul pities or learns or thinks, but that the man does so with the soul: and this, too, not in the sense that the motion occurs in the soul, but in the sense that motion sometimes reaches to, sometimes starts from, the soul. Thus, sensation originates in particular objects, while recollection, starting from the soul, is directed towards the movements or traces of movements in the sense-organs. But intellect would seem to be developed in us as a self-existing substance and to be imperishable, perishable. For, if anything could destroy it, it would be the feebleness of age. But, as things are, no doubt what occurs is the same as in the case of the sense-organs. If an aged man could procure an eye of the right sort, he would see just as well as a young man. Hence old age must be due to an affection or state not of the soul as such, but of that in which the soul resides, just as is the case in intoxication and disease. In like manner, then, thought and the exercise of knowledge are enfeebled through the loss of something else within, but are in themselves impassive. But reasoning, love and hatred are not attributes of the thinking faculty but of its individual possessor, in so far as he possesses it. Hence when this possessor perishes, there is neither memory nor love: for these never did belong to the thinking faculty, but to the composite whole which has perished, while the intellect is doubtless a thing more divine and is impassive.

From the foregoing it is clear that the soul is incapable of motion; and, if it is not moved at all, clearly it does not move criticism itself. Now of all the views that have been put forward by far the most irrational is that which makes the soul a self-moving number. Its supporters are involved in many impossibilities, not only in those which arise from attributing motion to the soul, but also in others of a special character due to calling it a number. For how are we to conceive of a unit, a thing which is without parts or differences, as in motion? By what would it be moved, and in what way? For if it is capable of imparting motion as well as of being moved, it must admit differences. Further, since they say that a line by its motion generates a surface and that a point by its motion generates a line, the movements of the units will also be lines, for a point is a unit having position. But the number of the soul must, from the nature of the case, be somewhere and have position. Again, if you subtract a number or unit from a number, a different number remains: whereas plants and many animals continue to live when divided and seem to have specifically the same soul in each segment. Besides, it would seem to make no difference whether we say units or tiny particles. For if the little round atoms of Democritus be converted into points and only their sum-total be retained, in such sum-total there will still be a part which moves and a part which is moved, just as there is in that which is extended. The truth of this statement does not depend upon the size of the atoms, whether great or small, but upon the fact that there is a sum-total or quantity of them. Hence there must be something to set the units in motion. But if in the animal the part which causes motion is the soul, then it is so likewise in the number: so that it will not be both that which causes motion and that which is moved which is the soul, but that which causes motion only. How then can this cause of motion be a unit? For if it were so there must be some difference between it and the other units. But what is there to differentiate points which are units, except position? If, then, the units, that is the points, in the body are distinct from the units of soul, the units of soul will be in the same place as the points, for each unit will occupy the space of a point. And yet if two things can be in the same place, why not an infinite number? When the place which things occupy is indivisible, the things themselves are also indivisible. If, on the other hand, the number of the soul consists of the points in the body, or if the soul is the number of such points, why are not all bodies possessed of soul? For in all bodies there would seem to be points: nay, an infinity of points. And, further, how can the points be separated and set free from the bodies to which they belong; unless, indeed, we are prepared to resolve lines into points?

Chapter 5

It comes to this, then, as we have said, first, that this view coincides with that which makes of the soul a body composed of fine particles; next, that its agreement with Democritus as to the manner in which he makes the body to be moved by the soul gives it an especial absurdity of its own. If the soul resides in the whole sentient body, on the assumption that the soul is a sort of body it necessarily follows that two bodies occupy the same space. Those who call the soul a number have to assume many points in the one point, or else that everything corporeal has a soul; unless the number that comes to exist in the body is a different number, quite distinct from the sum of the points already present in the body. Hence it follows that the animal is moved by the number in the same way precisely as we said Democritus moved it. For what difference does it make whether we speak of small round atoms or large units, or indeed of units in spatial motion at all? Either way it is necessary to make the motion of the animal depend on the motion of these atoms or units. Such, then, are some of the difficulties; confronting those who join motion and number: and there are many others, since it is impossible that the conjunction of motion with number should form even an attribute, much less the definition, of soul. This will be evident if we try to deduce from this definition the affections and functions of the soul; its reasonings, perceptions, pleasures, pains, and so forth. For, as we said above, from the account given it is difficult even to divine what these functions are.

Three modes of defining the soul have come down to us: some defined it as that which, in virtue of its self-motion, is most capable of causing motion; others as the body which consists of the finest particles, or which is more nearly incorporeal than anything else. And we have pretty fully explained what difficulties and inconsistencies these views present. It remains to consider what is meant by saying that the soul is composed of elements. Soul, we are told, is composed of the elements in order that it may perceive and know each several thing. But this theory necessarily involves many impossibilities. For it is assumed that like is known by like; which implies that soul is identical with the things that it knows. These elements, however, are not all that exists: there are a great, or perhaps we should say rather, an infinite number of other things as well, namely those which are compounded of the elements. Granted, then, that it is possible for the soul to know and to perceive the constituent elements of all these composite things, with what will it know or perceive the compound itself? I mean, what God or man is; what flesh or bone is: and so likewise with regard to any other composite thing. For it is not elements taken anyhow which constitute this or that thing, but only those which are united in a given proportion or combination, as Empedocles says of bone:

"Then did the bounteous earth in broad-bosomed crucibles win out of eight parts two from the sheen of moisture and four from the fire-god; and the bones came into being all white."

It is therefore of no use for the elements to be in the soul, unless it also contains their proportions and the mode of combining them. For each element will know its like, but there will be nothing to know bone or man, unless these also are to be present in the soul: which, I need hardly say, is impossible. Who would ask if stone or man resides in the soul? And similarly with that which is good and that which is not good: and so for all the rest.

Being, again, is a term which has various meanings, signifying sometimes the particular thing, sometimes the particular thing, sometimes quantity or quality or any of the other categories which have been already determined. Is the soul to be derived from all of these, or not? It cannot be: the general opinion is that there are no elements common to all the categories. Does the soul, then, consist of those elements alone which are the elements of substances? How then does it know each of the other categories? Or will they say that each summum genus has special elements and principles of its own, and that the soul is composed of these? Then soul will be at once quantity, quality and substance. But is it impossible from the elements of quantity to derive substance or anything but quantity. These, then, and others like them are the difficulties which confront those who derive soul from all the elements. There is a further inconsistency in maintaining that like is unaffected by like and yet at the same time that like perceives like and knows like by like. But they assume that perceiving is a sort of being acted upon or moved. And the same holds of thinking and knowing.

Of the many problems and difficulties involved in holding with Empedocles that each thing is known through corporeal elements and by reference to its like (what has just been said is evidence). For, it would seem, whatever within the bodies of animals consists entirely of earth, such as bones, sinews, hair, perceives nothing at all, and consequently cannot perceive its like; as in consistency it should. Moreover, each one of the elemental principles will have a far larger share of ignorance than of intelligence; there being many things of which it will be ignorant and only one which it will know: in fact, it will be ignorant of all besides that one. It follows, for Empedocles at any rate, that God is quite the most unintelligent of beings. There is one of the elements, viz. Strife, which he, and he alone, will not know, while mortal things, being composed of all the elements, will know them all. And in general, seeing that everything is either an element or derived from one or more or all elements, why should not all things that exist have soul? For they must certainly know one thing or some things or all. It might further be asked what it is that gives them unity. For the elements, at all events, correspond to matter. That other principle, whatever it be, which holds them together, is supreme. Yet it is impossible that anything should be superior to the soul and overrule it; and still more impossible that anything should overrule intelligence. This, it may reasonably be held, has a natural priority and authority. Yet we are told that the elements are prior to all other things that exist.

And it is characteristic, alike of those who derive the soul from the elements on the ground of perception and knowledge, and of those who define it as the thing most capable of causing motion, that their assertions do not apply to soul in every form. For not all sentient beings can cause motion; some animals are seen to be stationary in one place. And yet it is at all events a received view that this, namely, change of place, is the one form of motion which the soul imparts to the animal. Similarly with those who derive intelligence and the faculty of sense from the elements. For plants are found to live without any share in locomotion or sensation, and many animals to be destitute of thought. If we waive this point and assume intellect to be a part of the soul, and the faculty of sense likewise, even then their statements would not apply generally to all soul, nor to the whole of any one soul. The account given in the so-called Orphic poems is open to the same strictures. For the soul, it is there asserted, enters from the universe in the process of respiration, being borne upon the winds. Now it is impossible that this should be so with plants or even with some animals, seeing that they do not all respire: a point which the upholders of this theory have overlooked. And if the soul is to be constructed out of the elements, there is no need to employ them all, the one of a pair of contraries being sufficient to discern both itself and its opposite. For by that which is straight we discern both the straight and the crooked, the carpenter's rule being the test of both. On the other hand that which is crooked is not a test of itself or of that which is straight.

There are some, too, who say that soul is interfused throughout the universe: which is perhaps why Thales supposed things to be full of gods. But this view presents some difficulties. For why should the soul not produce an animal, when present in air or fire, and yet do so when present in the compounds of these elements: and that, too, though in the former case it is believed to be purer? One might also enquire why the soul present in air is purer and more immortal than soul in animals. Whichever of the two suppositions open to us we adopt is absurd and irrational. To speak of fire or air as an animal is very irrational; and on the other hand not to call them animals, if they contain soul, is absurd. But it would seem that the reason why they suppose soul to be in these elements is that the whole is homogeneous with its parts. So that they cannot help regarding universal soul as also homogeneous with the parts of it in animals, since it is through something of the surrounding element being cut off and enclosed in animals that the animals become endowed with soul. But if the air when split up remains homogeneous, and yet soul is divisible into non-homogeneous parts, it is clear that, although one part of soul may be present in the air, there is another part which is not. Either, then, soul must be homogeneous, or else it cannot be present in every part of the universe.

From what has been said it is evident that it is not because the soul is compounded of the elements that knowledge belongs to it, nor is it correct or true to say that the soul is moved. Knowledge, however, is an attribute of the soul, and so are perception, opinion, desire, wish and appetency generally; animal locomotion also is produced by the soul; and likewise growth, maturity and decay. Shall we then say that each of these belongs to the whole soul, that we think, that is, and perceive and are moved and in each of the other operations act and are acted upon with the whole soul, or that the different operations are to be assigned to different parts? And what of life itself? Does it reside in any single one or more or all of these parts? Or has it a cause entirely distinct? Now some say that the soul is divisible and that one part of it thinks, another desires. What is it then which holds the soul together, if naturally divisible? Assuredly it is not the body: on the contrary, the soul seems rather to hold the body together; at all events, when it has departed, the body disperses in air and rots away. If, then, the unity of soul is due to some other thing, that other thing would be, properly speaking, soul. We shall need, then, to repeat the enquiry respecting it also, whether it is one or manifold. For, if it has unity, why not attribute unity to the soul itself at the outset? If, however, it be divisible, then again reason will go on to ask what it is that holds it together, and so the enquiry will go on to infinity. It might also be asked what power each of the parts of the soul exercises in the body. For, if the entire soul holds together the whole body, then each of its parts ought properly to hold together some part of the body. But this seems impossible. For it is difficult even to conjecture what part the intellect will hold together or how it can hold any part together. It is found that plants, and among animals certain insects or annelida, live when divided, which implies that the soul in their segments is specifically, though not numerically, the same. At any rate, each of the two segments retains sentience and the power of locomotion for some time: that they do not continue to do so is not surprising, as they lack the organs requisite to maintain their nature. But none the less all the parts of the soul are contained in each of the two segments, and the two halves of the soul are homogeneous alike with one another and with the whole; a fact which implies that, while the parts of the soul are inseparable from one another, the soul as a whole is divisible. It would seem that the vital principle in plants also is a sort of soul. For this principle is the only one common to plants and animals; and, while it can be separated from the sensitive principle, no being which has sensation is without it.

BOOK II

Chapter 1

So much for the theories of soul handed down by our predecessors. Let us, then, make a fresh start and try to determine what soul is and what will be its most comprehensive definition. Now there is one class of existent things which we call substance, including under the term, firstly, matter, which in itself is not this or that; secondly, shape or form, in virtue of which the term this or that is at once applied; thirdly, the whole made up of matter and form. Matter is identical with potentiality, form with actuality. And there are two meanings of actuality: knowledge illustrates the one, exercise of knowledge the other. Now bodies above all things are held to be substances, particularly such bodies as are the work of nature; for to these all the rest owe their origin. Of natural bodies some possess life and some do not: where by life we mean the power of self-nourishment and of independent growth and decay. Consequently every natural body possessed of life must be substance, and substance of the composite order. And since in fact we have here body with a certain attribute, namely, the possession of life, the body will not be the soul: for the body is not an attribute of a subject, it stands rather for a subject of attributes, that is, matter. It must follow, then, that soul is substance in the sense that it is the form of a natural body having in it the capacity of life. Such substance is actuality. The soul, therefore, is the actuality of the body above described. But the term 'actuality' is used in two senses; in the one it answers to knowledge, in the other to the exercise of knowledge. Clearly in this case it is analogous to knowledge:

for sleep, as well as waking, implies the presence of soul; and, whilst waking is analogous to the exercise of knowledge, sleep is analogous to the possession of knowledge without its exercise; and in the same individual the possession of knowledge comes in order of time before its exercise. Hence soul is the first actuality of a natural body having in it the capacity of life. And a body which is possessed of organs answers to this description. We may note that the parts of plants, as well as those of animals, are organs, though of a very simple sort: for instance, a leaf is the sheath of the pod and the pod of the fruit. The roots, again, are analogous to the mouths of animals, both serving to take in nourishment. If, then, we have to make a general statement touching soul in all its forms, the soul will be the first actuality of a natural body furnished with organs. Hence there is no need to enquire whether soul and body are one, any more than whether the wax and the imprint are one; or, in general, whether the matter of a thing is the same with that of which it is the matter. For, of all the various meanings borne by the terms unity and being, actuality is the meaning which belongs to them by the fullest right.

It has now been stated in general terms what soul is, namely, substance as notion or form. And this is the quiddity of such and such a body. Suppose, for example, that any instrument, an axe, were a natural body, its axeity would be its substance, would in fact be its soul. If this were taken away, it would cease, except in an equivocal sense, to be an axe. But the axe is after all an axe. For it is not of a body of this kind that the soul is the quiddity, that is, the notion or form, but of a natural body of a particular sort, having in itself the origination of motion and rest.

Further, we must view our statement in the light of the parts of the body. For, if the eye were an animal, eyesight would be its soul, this being the substance as notion or form of the eye. The eye is the matter of eyesight, and in default of eyesight it is no longer an eye, except equivocally, like an eye in stone or in a picture. What has been said of the part must be understood to apply to the whole living body; for, as the sensation of a part of the body is to that part, so is sensation as .a whole to the whole sentient body as such. By that which has in it the capacity of life is meant not the body which has lost its soul, but that which possesses it. Now the seed in animals, like the fruit in plants, is that which is potentially such and such a body. As, then, the cutting of the axe or the seeing of the eye is full actuality, so, too, is the waking state; while the soul is actuality in the same sense as eyesight and the capacity of the instrument. The body, on the other hand, is simply that which is potentially existent. But, just as in the one case the eye means the pupil in conjunction with the eyesight, so in the other soul and body together constitute the animal.

Now it needs no proof that the soul - or if it is divisible into parts, certain of its parts - cannot be separated from the separable body, for there are cases where the actuality belongs to the parts themselves. There is, however, no reason why some parts should not be separated, if they are not the actualities of any body whatever. Again, it is not clear whether the soul may not be the actuality of the body as the sailor is of the ship. This, then, may suffice for an outline or provisional sketch of soul.

Chapter 2

But, as it is from the things which are naturally obscure, though more easily recognised by us, that we proceed to what is clear and, in the order of thought, more knowable, we must employ this method in trying to give a fresh account of soul. For it is not enough that the defining statement should set forth the fact, as most definitions do; it should also contain and present the cause: whereas in practice what is stated in the definition is usually no more than a conclusion. For example, what is quadrature? The construction of an equilateral rectangle equal in area to a given oblong. But such a definition expresses merely the conclusion. Whereas, if you say that quadrature is the discovery of a mean proportional, then you state the reason.

We take, then, as our starting-point for discussion that it is life which distinguishes the animate from the inanimate. But the term life is used in various senses; and, if life is present in but a single one of these senses, we speak of a thing as living. Thus there is intellect, sensation, motion from place to place and rest, the motion concerned with nutrition and, operations, further, decay and growth. Hence it is that all plants are supposed to have life. For apparently they have within themselves a faculty and principle whereby they grow and decay in opposite directions. For plants do not grow upwards without growing downwards; they grow in both directions equally, in fact in all directions, as many as are constantly nourished and therefore continue to live, so long as they are capable of absorbing nutriment. This form of life can be separated from the others, though in mortal creatures the others cannot be separated from it. In the case of plants the fact is manifest: for they have no other faculty of soul at all.

It is, then, in virtue of this principle that all living things live, whether animals or plants. But it is sensation primarily which constitutes the animal. For, provided they have sensation, even those creatures which are devoid of movement and do not change their place are called animals and are not merely said to be alive. Now the primary sense in all animals is touch. But, as the nutritive faculty may exist without touch or any form of sensation, so also touch may exist apart from the other senses. By nutritive faculty we mean the part of the soul in which even plants share. Animals, however, are found universally to have the sense of touch: why this is so in each of the two cases will be stated hereafter.

For the present it may suffice to say that the soul is the origin of the functions above enumerated and is determined by them, namely, by capacities of nutrition, sensation, thought, and by motion. But whether each one of these is a soul or part of a soul and, if a part, whether it is only logically distinct or separable in space also is a question, the answer to which is in some cases not hard to see: other cases present difficulties. For, just as in the case of plants some of them are found to live when divided and separated from each other (which implies that the soul in each plant, though actually one, is potentially several souls), so, too, when insects or annelida are cut up, we see the same thing happen with other varieties of soul: I mean, each of the segments has sensation and moves from place to place, and, if it has sensation, it has also imagination and appetency. For, where there is sensation, there is also pleasure and pain: and, where these are, desire also must of necessity be present. But as regards intellect and the speculative faculty the case is not yet clear. It would seem, however, to be a distinct species of soul, and it alone is capable of separation from the body, as that which is eternal from that which is perishable. The remaining parts of the soul are, as the foregoing consideration shows, not separable in the way that some allege them to be: at the same time it is clear that they are logically distinct. For the faculties of sensation and of opinion taken in the abstract are distinct, since to have sensation and to opine are distinct. And so it is likewise with each of the other faculties above mentioned. Again, while some animals possess all these functions, others have only some of them, others only one. It is this which will differentiate animal from animal. The reason why this is so must be investigated hereafter. The case is similar with the several senses: some animals have all of them, others some of them, others again only one, the most indispensable, that is, touch.

Now "that by which we live and have sensation" is a phrase a with two meanings, answering to the two meanings of "that by which we know" (the latter phrase means, firstly, knowledge and, secondly, soul, by either of which we say we know). Similarly that by which we have health means either health itself or a certain part, if not the whole, of the body. Now of these knowledge and health are the shape and in some sort form, the notion and virtual activity, of that which is capable of receiving in the one case knowledge, in the other health: that is to say, it is in that which is acted upon or conditioned that the activity of the causal agencies would seem to take effect. Now the soul is that whereby primarily we live, perceive, and have understanding: therefore it will be a species of notion or form, not matter or substratum. Of the three meaning's of substance mentioned above, form, matter and the whole made up of these two, matter is potentiality and form is actuality. And, since the whole made up of the two is endowed with soul, the body is not the actuality of soul, but soul the actuality of a particular body. Hence those are right who regard the soul as not independent of body and yet at the same time as not itself a species of body. It is not body, but something belonging to body, and therefore resides in body and, what is more, in such and such a body. Our predecessors were wrong in endeavouring to fit the soul into a body without further determination of the nature and qualities of that body: although we do not even find that of any two things taken at random the one will admit the other. And this result is what we might expect. For the actuality of each thing comes naturally to be developed in the potentiality of each thing: in other words, in the appropriate matter. From these considerations, then, it is manifest that soul is a certain actuality, a notion or form, of that which has the capacity to be endowed with soul.

Chapter 3

Of the powers of soul above mentioned, namely, those of nutrition, appetency, sensation, locomotion and understanding, some living things, as we remarked, possess all, others some, others again only one. Plants possess the nutritive faculty only: other things along with this have sensation; and, if sensation, then also appetency: where under appetency we include desire, anger and wish. But all animals have at least one sense, touch: and, where sensation is found, there is pleasure and pain, and that which causes pleasure and pain; and, where these are, there also is desire, desire being appetite for what is pleasurable. Again, they have a sensation concerned with nutriment, touch being such a sense. For it is by what is dry and moist, hot and cold, that all living things are nourished (and these qualities are perceived by touch, whereas the other sensibles are not, except incidentally): for sound, colour and odour contribute nothing to nutriment, while flavour is one of the tangible objects. Hunger again, and thirst are forms of desire, the one for what is hot or dry, the other for what is cold or moist. Flavour is, as it were, the seasoning of these. We will deal with these in detail hereafter: at present let it suffice to say that all animals which have the sense of touch are also endowed with appetency. Whether they have imagination is not clear: this, too, must be considered later. Some have in addition the power of locomotion. Others - that is to say, man and any other species like man or, possibly, superior to him - have also the thinking faculty and intellect.

From this it is clear that there is one definition of soul exactly as there is one definition of figure: for there is in the one case no figure excepting triangle, quadrilateral and the rest, nor is there in the other any species of soul apart from those above mentioned. Again, a definition might be constructed which should apply to all figures, but not specially to any species of figure. And similarly with the species of soul above enumerated. Hence it would be absurd here as elsewhere to seek a general definition which will not be properly a definition of anything in existence and will not be applicable to the particular irreducible species before us, to the neglect of the definition which is so applicable.

The types of soul resemble the series of figures. For, alike in figures and in things animate, the earlier form exists potentially in the later, as, for instance, the triangle potentially in the quadrilateral, and the nutritive faculty in that which has sensation. So that we must examine in each case separately, what is the soul of plant, of man or of beast. Why they are related in this order of succession remains to be considered. There is no sensitive faculty apart from the nutritive: and yet the latter exists without the former in plants. Again, none of the other senses is found apart from touch; while touch is found apart from the others, many animals having neither sight nor hearing nor sense of smell. Also of those which possess sensation, some can move from place to place, others cannot. Lastly and most rarely, they have the reasoning faculty and thought. For those perishable creatures which possess reason are endowed with all the other species of soul, but not all those which possess each of the other faculties have reason. Indeed, some of them have not even imagination, while others live by imagination alone. As for the speculative intellect, it calls for a separate discussion. Meanwhile it is clear that an account of the several faculties is at the same time the most appropriate account of soul.

Chapter 4

The enquirer who approaches this subject must ascertain what order of each of these faculties is before he proceeds to investigate the questions next in order and so forth. But if we are asked to state what each of these is; that is to say, what the cognitive, sensitive and nutritive faculties respectively are, we must begin by stating what the act of thinking is and what the act of sensation is. For activities and functions are logically prior to faculties. But, if so, and if a study of the correlative objects should have preceded, these objects will for the same reason have to be defined first: I mean, nutriment and the sensible and intelligible. Consequently we have first to treat of nutriment and of generation.

The nutritive soul belongs to other living things as well as man, being the first and most widely distributed faculty, in virtue of which all things possess life. Its functions are reproduction and assimilation of nutriment. For it is the most natural function in all living things, if perfect and not defective or spontaneously generated, to reproduce their species; animal producing animal and plant plant, in order that they may, so far as they can, share in the eternal and the divine. For it is that which all things yearn after, and that is the final cause of all their natural activity. Here final cause is an ambiguous term, which denotes either the purpose for which, or the person for whom, a thing is done. Since, then, individual things are incapable of sharing continuously in the eternal and the divine, because nothing in the world of perishables can abide numerically one. and the same, they partake in the eternal and divine, each in the only way it can, some more, some less. That is to say, each persists, though not in itself, yet in a representative which is specifically, not numerically, one with it.

Now the soul is cause and origin of the living body. But cause and origin are terms used in various senses: accordingly soul is cause in the three senses of the word already determined. For the soul is the cause of animate bodies as being in itself the origin of motion, as final cause and as substance. Clearly it is so as substance, substance being the cause of all existence. And for living things existence means life, and it is the soul which is the cause and origin of life. Furthermore, actuality is the notion or form of that which has potential existence. Manifestly, too, the soul is final cause. For nature, like intelligence, acts for a purpose, and this purpose is for it an end. Such an end the soul is in animals, and this in the order of nature, for all the natural bodies are instruments of soul: and this is as true of the bodies of plants as of those of animals, showing that all are means to the soul as end; where end has two senses, the purpose for which and the person for whom. Moreover, the soul is also the origin of motion from place to place, but not all living things have this power of locomotion. Qualitative change, also, and growth are due to soul. For sensation is supposed to be a sort of qualitative change, and nothing devoid of soul has sensation. The same holds of growth and decay. For nothing undergoes natural decay or growth except it be nourished, and nothing is nourished unless it shares in life.

Empedocles is mistaken in adding that in plants, in so far as they strike their roots downwards, growth takes place because the earth in them has a natural tendency in this direction and that, when they shoot upwards, it is because the fire in them has a similar tendency upwards. He is wrong in his view of up and down. For up and down are not the same for all individuals as for the universe. On the contrary, the roots of plants correspond to the heads of animals, if we are to make identity and diversity of organs depend upon their functions. Besides, what is it that holds together the fire and the earth, tending, as they do, in opposite directions? For they will be rent asunder, unless there is something to prevent it: while, if there is, it is this which is the soul and the cause of growth and nourishment.

Some hold the nature of fire to be singly and solely the cause of nourishment and growth. For it would seem that fire is the only body or element which of itself is nourished and grows. Hence fire might be supposed to be the operative cause, both in plants and animals. Whereas, though it is in a sense a joint cause, it is not a cause absolutely: it is rather the soul which is so. For fire goes on growing to infinity, as long as there is fuel to be consumed, but in natural wholes there is always a limit or proportion which determines growth and size. But this belongs to the soul and not to fire, to form rather than to matter.

The nutritive faculty of the soul being the same as the reproductive, it is necessary first to give a definition of nutriment. For it is by the nutritive function that this faculty is separated off from the others. The common view is that contrary is nutriment to contrary; though not in every case, but wherever each of two contraries is not only generated by, but derives growth from, the other. For many things are derived from one another, but not all of them are quantities: thus the sick man becomes well. But it is found that even the contraries supposed to derive growth from each other are not fed by one another in the same way: while water serves to feed fire, fire is not nutriment to water. It would seem, then, that it is in the simple bodies above all that of two contraries one is nutriment and the other is nourished. Yet here is a difficulty. It is said by the one side that like is nourished by, as well as derives its growth from, like; while the others, again, as we explained, hold that contrary is nourished by contrary, on the ground that like cannot be affected by like, while food undergoes change and is digested. Now change is always in the direction of the opposite, or of the intermediate state. Further, nutriment is acted upon by that which it nourishes, and not the latter by the former: just as the carpenter is not affected by his material, but on the contrary the material by the carpenter. The carpenter merely passes to activity from inaction. But it makes a difference whether by nutriment we mean the final, or the primary, form of what is added. If both are nutriment, the one as undigested, the other as digested, it will be possible to use the term nutriment in conformity with both theories. For, in so far as it is undigested, contrary is nourished by contrary: and, in so far as it is digested, like by like. So that clearly both sides are in a manner partly right and partly wrong. But, since nothing is nourished unless it possesses life, that which is nourished must be the animate body as such: so that nutriment also is relative to the animate being which it nourishes: and this not incidentally merely.

There is, however, a difference between nutritivity and conducivity to growth. In so far as the animate thing is quantitative, what is taken promotes growth; in so far as it is a definite individual, what is taken nourishes. For the animate thing preserves its substance or essential nature and exists as long as it is nourished: and it causes the production, not of that which is nourished, but of another individual like it. Its essential nature already exists, and nothing generates itself, it only maintains its existence. Hence the above described principle of the soul is the power to preserve in existence that which possesses it in so far as it is a definite individual, while nutrition prepares it for activity. Therefore it cannot live when deprived of nutriment. There are, then, these three things, that which is nourished, that with which it is nourished, and that which nourishes it. The last of the three is the primary soul, that which is nourished is the body which contains the soul, that wherewith it is nourished is nutriment. As, however, it is right to name all things from the end they subserve, and the end here is reproduction of the species, the primary soul is that which is capable of reproducing the species. That with which the living thing is nourished may be understood in two senses, just as that with which one steers may mean the hand or the rudder; the former, the hand, both causing motion and being moved, the latter, the rudder, being simply moved. Now it is necessary that all food should be capable of digestion, and digestion is promoted by heat; this explains why every animate thing has warmth. This, then, is an outline of what nutriment is. It must be more clearly defined hereafter in the discussion devoted specially to it.

Chapter 5

Now that these points have been determined, let us proceed to a general discussion of all sensation. As above remarked, sensation consists in being moved and acted upon, for it is held to be a species of qualitative change. Some add that like is in fact acted upon by like. How far this is possible or impossible we have explained in the general discussion of action and passivity. The question arises why there is no sensation of the senses themselves: that is, why they produce no sensation apart from external sensibles, though the senses contain fire, earth and the other elements, which are the objects of sensation either in themselves or through their attributes. Evidently it follows that the faculty of sensible perception exists not in activity, but only in potentiality. Hence it must be here as with the fuel which does not burn of and in itself without something to make it burn; otherwise it would kindle itself and would have no need of the fire which is actually existent. Now to have sensation has two meanings: we use the terms hearing and seeing of that which has the capacity to hear and see, even though it be at the time asleep, just as we do of that which already actually hears and sees. And therefore sensation, too, will have two meanings: it may mean either potential or actual sensation. Similarly with having sensation, whether potential or actual.

Let us then first proceed on the assumption that to be acted upon or moved is identical with active operation. For movement is in fact active operation of some sort, though incomplete, as we have elsewhere explained. But in every case things are acted upon and moved by an agent in actual operation. It follows that in one sense what is acted upon is acted upon by what is like it, in another sense by what is unlike it, as we have explained. That is to say, while being acted upon it is unlike, after it has been acted upon, it is like the agent.

We must also draw a distinction in regard to the terms potentiality and actuality: at present we are using them without qualification. For instance, we may use the term wise, firstly, in the sense in which we might speak of man as wise because man is one of the genus of beings which are wise and have wisdom; secondly, in the sense in which we at once call the man wise who has learnt, say, grammar. Now of these two men each possesses the capacity, but in a different sense: the one because the genus to which he belongs, that is to say, his matter, is potentially wise; the other because he is capable, if he chose, of applying the wisdom he has acquired, provided there is nothing external to hinder. Whereas he who is at the moment exercising his wisdom is in actuality and is wise in the proper sense of the term: for example, he knows the A before him. Thus the first two are both potentially wise: the first becomes wise actually after he has undergone qualitative change through instruction and often after transition from the reverse condition; while in the latter case it is by another kind of transition that the man passes from the mere possession, without the use, of sensation or grammar to the use of it.

To suffer or be acted upon, too, is a term of more than one meaning. Sometimes it means a sort of destruction by the contrary, sometimes it is rather a preservation of what is potentially existent by what is actually existent and like it, so far as likeness holds of potentiality when compared with actuality. For it is by exercise of knowledge that the possessor of knowledge becomes such in actuality: and this either is no qualitative change (for the thing develops into its own nature and actuality), or else is qualitative change of a different sort. Hence it is not right to say that that which thinks undergoes change when it thinks, any more than that the builder undergoes change when he builds. That, then, which works the change from potential existence to actuality in a thinking and intelligent being should properly receive a different name and not be called instruction: while that which learns and is brought from potential to actual knowledge by that which is in actuality and capable of instructing should either not be said to suffer or be acted upon at all, or else two modes of change should be assumed, one to the negative states and the other to the normal habits and the true nature.

Chapter 6

In the sensitive subject the first change is due to the parent: once generated it possesses sensation exactly in the same sense as we possess knowledge. And to have actual sensation corresponds to exercise of knowledge. There is this difference, however, that in the one case the causes of the activity are external: as, for instance, the objects of sight, hearing and the other senses. The reason is that actual sensation is always of particulars, while knowledge is of universals: and these universals are, in a manner, in the soul itself. Hence it is in our power to think whenever we please, but sensation is not in our power: for the presence of the sensible object is necessary. It is much the same with the sciences which deal with sensible objects; and for the same reason, namely, that sensibles are particulars and are external.

But we shall have a further opportunity of making this clear hereafter. For the present let us be content to have established that of the two meanings of potentiality, the one according to which a child might be called potentially a general, and the other according to which a man of full age might be so called, it is the latter which applies to the faculty of sense-perception. But as this distinction has no word to mark it, although the fact and the nature of the distinction have been established, we are compelled to use the terms to suffer or be acted upon and to be qualitatively changed as if they were the proper terms. Now, as has been explained, the sensitive faculty is potentially such as the sensible object is in actuality. While it is being acted upon, it is not yet similar, but, when once it has been acted upon, it is assimilated and has the same character as the sensible object.

In considering each separate sense we must first treat of their objects. By the sensible object may be meant any one of three things, two of which we say are perceived in themselves or directly, while the third is perceived *per accidens* or indirectly. Of the first two the one is the special object of a particular sense, the other an object common to all the senses. By a special object of a particular sense I mean that which cannot be perceived by any other sense and in respect to which deception is impossible; for example, sight is of colour, hearing of sound and taste of flavour, while touch no doubt has for its object several varieties. But at any rate each single sense judges of its proper objects and is not deceived as to the fact that there is a colour or a sound; though as to what or where the coloured object is or what or where the object is which produces the sound, mistake is possible Such then, are the special objects of the several senses. By common sensibles are meant motion, rest, number, figure, size: for such qualities are not the special objects of any single sense, but are common to all. For example, a particular motion can be perceived by touch as well as by sight. What is meant by the indirect object of sense may be illustrated if we suppose that the white thing before you is Diares' son. You perceive Diares' son, but indirectly, for that which you perceive is accessory to the whiteness. Hence you are not affected by the indirect sensible as such. Of the two classes of sensibles directly perceived it is the objects special to the different senses which are properly perceptible: and it is to these that the essential character of each sense is naturally adapted.

Chapter 7

The object, then, of sight is the visible: what is visible is colour and something besides which can be described, though it has no name. What we mean will best be made clear as we proceed. The visible, then, is colour. Now colour is that with which what is visible in itself is overlaid: and, when I say in itself, I do not mean what is visible by its essence or form, but what is visible because it contains within itself the cause of visibility, namely, colour. But colour is universally capable of exciting change in the actually transparent, that is, in light; this being, in fact, the true nature of colour. Hence colour is not visible without light, but the colour of each object is always seen in light. And so we shall have first to explain what light is.

There is, then, we assume, something transparent; and by this I mean that which, though visible, is not properly speaking, visible in itself, but by reason of extrinsic colour. Air, water and many solid bodies answer to this description. For they are not transparent *quâ* air or *quâ* water, but because there is a certain natural attribute present in both of them which is present also in the eternal body on high. Light is the actuality of this transparent *quâ* transparent. But where the transparent is only potentially present, there darkness is actually. Light is a sort of colour in the transparent when made transparent in actuality by the agency of fire or something resembling the celestial body: for this body also has an attribute which is one and the same with that of fire. What the transparent is, and what light is, has now been stated; namely, that it is neither fire nor body generally nor an effluence from any body (for even then it would still be a sort of body), but the presence of fire or something fiery in the transparent. For it is impossible for two bodies to occupy the same space at the same time.

Light is held to be contrary to darkness. But darkness is absence from the transparent of the quality above described: so that plainly light is the presence of it. Thus Empedocles and others who propounded the same view are wrong when they represent light as moving in space and arriving at a given point of time between the earth and that which surrounds it without our perceiving its motion. For this contradicts not only the clear evidence of reason, but also the facts of observation: since, though a movement of light might elude observation within a short distance, that it should do so all the way from east to west is too much to assume.

It is that which is colourless which is receptive of colour, as it is that which is soundless which is receptive of sound. And the transparent is colourless, and so is the invisible or the dimly visible which is our idea of the dark. Such is the transparent medium, not indeed when it is in actuality, but when potentially transparent. For it is the same natural attribute which is at one time darkness and at another time light. It is not everything visible which is visible in light, but only the proper colour of each thing. Some things, indeed, are not seen in daylight, though they produce sensation in the dark: as, for example, the things of fiery and glittering appearance, for which there is no one distinguishing name, like fungus, horn, the heads, scales and eyes of fishes. But in no one of these cases is the proper colour seen. Why these objects are seen must be discussed elsewhere. At present this much is clear, that the object seen in light is colour, and this is why it is not seen without light. For the very quiddity of colour is, as we saw, just this, that it is capable of exciting change in the operantly transparent medium: and the activity of the transparent is light. There is clear evidence of this. If you lay the coloured object upon your eye, you will not see it. On the contrary, what the colour excites is the transparent medium, say, the air, and by this, which is continuous, the sense-organ is stimulated. For it was a mistake in Democritus to suppose that if the intervening space became a void, of a even an ant would be distinctly seen, supposing there were one in the sky. That is impossible. For sight takes place through an affection of the sensitive faculty. Now it cannot be affected by that which is seen, the colour itself: therefore it can only be by the intervening medium: hence the existence of some medium is necessary. But, if the intermediate space became a void, so far from being seen distinctly, an object would not be visible at all.

We have explained the reason why colour must be seen in light. Fire is visible both in light and in darkness: and necessarily so, for it is owing to fire that the transparent becomes transparent. The same argument holds for sound and odour. For no sound or scent produces sensation by contact with the sense-organ: it is the intervening medium which is excited by sound and odour and the respective sense-organs by the medium. But, when the body which emits the sound or odour is placed on the sense-organ itself, it will not produce any sensation. The same holds of touch and taste, although it appears to be otherwise. The reason for this will be seen hereafter. The medium for sounds is air, that for odour has no name. For there is assuredly a common quality in air and water, and this quality, which is present in both, stands to the body which emits odour in the same relation as the transparent to colour. For the animals that live in water also appear to have the sense of smell. But man and the other land-animals which breathe are unable to smell without inhaling breath. The reason for this, too, must be reserved for future explanation.

Chapter 8

Let us now begin by determining the nature of sound and hearing. There are two sorts of sound, one a sound which is operant, the other potential sound. For some things we say have no sound, as sponge, wool; others, for example, bronze and all things solid and smooth, we say have sound, because they can emit sound, that is, they can produce actual sound between the sonorous body and the organ of hearing. When actual sound occurs it is always of something on something and in something, for it is a blow which produces it. Hence it is impossible that a sound should be produced by a single thing, for, as that which strikes is distinct from that which is struck, that which sounds sounds upon something. And a blow implies spatial motion. As we stated above, it is not concussion of any two things taken at random which constitutes sound. Wool, when struck, emits no sound at all, but bronze does, and so do all smooth and hollow things; bronze emits sound because it is smooth, while hollow things by reverberation produce a series of concussions after the first, that which is set in motion being unable to escape.

Further, sound is heard in air and, though more faintly, in water. It is not the air or the water, however, which chiefly determine the production of sound: on the contrary, there must be solid bodies colliding with one another and with the air: and this happens when the air after being struck resists the impact and is not dispersed. Hence the air must be struck quickly and forcibly if it is to give forth sound; for the movement of the striker must be too rapid to allow the air time to disperse: just as would be necessary if one aimed a blow at a heap of sand or a sand whirl, while it was in rapid motion onwards.

Echo is produced when the air is made to rebound backwards like a ball from some other air which has become a single mass owing to its being within a cavity which confines it and prevents its dispersion. It seems likely that echo is always produced, but is not always distinctly audible: since surely the same thing happens with sound as with light For light is always being reflected; else light would not be everywhere, but outside the spot where the sun's rays fall there would be darkness. But it is not always reflected in the same way as it is from water or bronze or any other smooth surface; I mean, it does not always produce the shadow, by which we define light.

Void is rightly stated to be the indispensable condition of hearing. For the air is commonly believed to be a void, and it is the air which causes hearing, when being one and continuous it is set in motion. But, owing to its tendency to disperse, it gives out no sound unless that which is struck is smooth. In that case the air when struck is simultaneously reunited because of the unity of the surface; for a smooth body presents a single surface.

That, then, is resonant which is capable of exciting motion in a mass of air continuously one as far as the ear. There is air naturally attached to the ear. And because the ear is in air, when the external air is set in motion, the air within the ear moves. Hence it is not at every point that the animal hears, nor that the air passes through: for it is not at every point that the part which is to set itself in motion and to be animate has a supply of air. Of itself, then, the air is a soundless thing because it is easily broken up. But, whenever it is prevented from breaking up, its movement is sound. But the air within the ears has been lodged fast within walls to make it immoveable, in order that it may perceive exactly all the varieties of auditory movement. This is why we hear in water also, because the water does not pass right up to the air attached to the ear, nor even into the ear at all, because of its convolutions. Should this happen, hearing is destroyed, as it is by an injury to the membrane of the tympanum, and as sight is by an injury to the cornea. Further, we have evidence whether we hear or not, according as there is or is not always a ringing sound in the ears, as in a horn: for the air imprisoned there is always moving with a proper motion of its own. But sound is something of external origin and is not native to the ear. And this is why it is said that we hear by means of what is empty and resonant, because that by which we hear has air confined within it.

Does that which is struck emit the sound or that which strikes? Is it not rather both, but each in a different way? For sound is motion of that which is capable of being moved in the same manner as things rebound from smooth surfaces when struck sharply against them. Thus, as above remarked, it is not everything which, when struck or striking, emits sound: supposing, for instance, a pin were to strike against a pin, there would be no sound. The thing struck must be of even surface, so that the air may rebound and vibrate in one mass.

The varieties of resonant bodies are clearly distinguished by the sound they actually emit. For, as without light colours are not seen, so without sound we cannot distinguish high and low or acute and grave in pitch. These latter terms are used by analogy from tangible objects. For the acute, that is, the high, note moves the sense much in a little time, while the grave or low note moves it little in much time. Not that what is shrill is identically rapid, nor what is low is slow, but it is in the one case the rapidity, in the other the slowness, which makes the motion or sensation such as has been described. And it would seem that there is a certain analogy between the acute and grave to the ear and the acute and blunt to the touch. For that which is acute or pointed, as it were, stabs, while the blunt, as it were, thrusts, because the one excites motion in a short, the other in a long time, so that *per accidens* the one is quick, the other slow. Let this account of sound suffice.

Voice is a sound made by an animate being. No inanimate thing is vocal, though it may by analogy be said to be vocal, as in the case of the pipe, the lyre and all other inanimate things that have pitch and tune and articulation: for these qualities, it would seem, the voice also possesses. But many animals have no voice: that is to say, all bloodless animals and, among animals that have blood, fishes. And this is what we might expect, since sound is a movement of air. Those fishes which are said to possess voice, such as those in the Achelous, merely make a noise with their gills or some other such part. Voice is sound made by an animal, and not by any part of its body indifferently. But, as in every case of sound there is something that strikes, something struck and a medium, which is air, it is reasonable that only creatures which inhale air should have voice. For here nature uses the air that is inhaled for two purposes, just as it uses the tongue for tasting and for speech, the former use, for tasting, being indispensable and therefore more widely found, while expression of thought is a means to well-being. Similarly nature uses the breath first as a necessary means to the maintenance of internal warmth (the reason for which shall be explained elsewhere) and, further, as a means of producing voice and so promoting well-being. The organ of respiration is the larynx, and the part to which this part is subservient is the lung: for it is this organ, namely, the lung, which enables land animals to maintain a higher temperature than others. Respiration is also needed primarily for the region about the heart. Hence, as we draw breath, the air enters: and so the impact upon the windpipe, as it is called, of the air breathed is voice, the cause of the impact being the soul which animates the vocal organs. For, as we said before, it is not every sound made by an animal that is voice. Noise can be produced even with the tongue or as in coughing: but it is necessary for voice that the part which strikes should be animate and that some mental image should be present. For voice is certainly a sound which has significance and is not like a cough, the noise of air respired: rather with this air the animal makes the air in the windpipe strike against the windpipe. A proof of this is the fact that we cannot speak while inhaling or exhaling breath, but only while we hold it in: for anyone who holds his breath uses the breath so held to cause motion. And it is evident why fishes are voiceless. It is because they have no larynx. And they are without this part because they do not take in the air nor breathe. Why this is so does not concern us here.

Chapter 9

Of smell and the object of smell it is less easy to speak definitely than of the senses above-mentioned: for the nature of odour is by no means so clear as is the nature of sound or of colour. The reason is that this sense in us is not exact, but in inferior to that of many animals. In fact, man has man a poor olfactory sense and perceives none of the objects of smell unless they be painful or pleasant, which implies that the organ is wanting in accuracy. It is reasonable to suppose that animals with hard eyes perceive colour in the same vague way and do not distinguish the varieties of colour except in so far as they do, or do not, inspire fear. And this is the way in which mankind perceive odours. For it would seem that, while there is an analogy to taste and the varieties of flavour answer to the varieties of smell, our sense of taste is more exact because it is a modification of touch and the sense of touch is the most exact of man's senses. In the other senses man is inferior to many of the animals, but in delicacy of touch he is far superior to the rest. And to this he owes his superior intelligence. This may be seen from the fact-that it is this organ of sense and nothing else which makes all the difference in the human race between the natural endowments of man and man. For hard-skinned men are dull of intellect, while those who are soft-skinned are gifted.

As with flavours, so with odours: some are sweet, some bitter. (But in some objects smell and flavour correspond; for example, they have sweet odour and sweet flavour: in other things the opposite is the case.) Similarly, too, an odour may be pungent, irritant, acid or oily. But because, as we said above, odours are not as clearly defined as the corresponding flavours, it is from these latter that the odours have taken their names, in virtue of the resemblance in the things. Thus the odour of saffron and honey is sweet, while the odour of thyme and the like is pungent; and so in all the other cases. Again, smell corresponds to hearing and to each of the other 4 senses in that, as hearing is of the audible and inaudible, and sight of the visible and invisible, so smell is of the odorous and inodorous. By inodorous may be meant either that which is wholly incapable of having odour or that which has a slight or faint odour. The term tasteless involves a similar ambiguity.

Further, smell also operates through a medium, namely, air or water. For water animals, too, whether they are, or are not, possessed of blood, seem to perceive odour as much as the creatures in the air: since some of them also come from a great distance to seek their food, guided by the scent.

Hence there is an obvious difficulty, if the process of smell is everywhere the same, and yet man smells when inhaling but does not smell when instead of inhaling he is exhaling or holding his breath, no matter whether the object be distant or near, or even if it be placed on the inside of the nostril. The inability to perceive what is placed immediately on the sense-organ man shares with all animals: what is peculiar to him is that he cannot smell without inhaling. This is made plain by experiment. Consequently bloodless animals, since they do not breathe, might be thought to have a distinct sense other than those commonly recognised. But, we reply, that is impossible, since it is odour which they perceive. For perception of odour, be it fragrant or noisome, constitutes smelling. Moreover, it is found that these bloodless animals are destroyed by the same powerful odours as man, such as asphalt, brimstone and the like. It follows then that they do smell, but not by inhaling breath.

It would seem, again, that in man the organ of this sense differs from that of the other animals, as his eyes differ from those of hard-eyed animals. Man's eyes have, in the eyelids, a sort of screen or sheath and without moving or opening them he cannot see: while the hard-eyed animals have nothing of the kind, but at once see whatever is taking place in the transparent medium. So, too, it seems, the organ of smell in some animals is unenclosed, just as is the eye, but in those which take in the air it has a curtain, which is removed in the process of inhaling, by dilatation of the veins and passages. And this is the reason why animals which breathe cannot smell in the water. For it is necessary for them to take in breath before smelling and this they cannot do in the water. Odour is included under that which is dry, as flavour under that which is moist, and the organ of smell is potentially dry also.

Chapter 10

The object of taste is a species of tangible. And this is the reason why it is not perceived through a foreign body as medium: for touch employs no such medium either. The body, too, in which the flavour resides, the proper object of taste, has the moist, which is something tangible, for its matter or vehicle. Hence, even if we lived in water, we should still perceive anything sweet thrown into the water, but our perception would not have come through the medium, but by the admixture of sweetness with the fluid, as is the case with what we drink. But it is not in this way, namely, by admixture, that colour is perceived, nor yet by emanations. Nothing, then, corresponds to the medium; but to colour, which is the object of sight, corresponds the flavour, which is the object of taste. But nothing produces perception of flavour in the absence of moisture, but either actually or potentially the producing cause must have liquid in it: salt, for instance, for that is easily dissolved and acts as a dissolvent upon the tongue.

Again, sight is of the invisible as well as the visible (for darkness is invisible and this, too, sight discerns as well as light) and, further, of that which is exceedingly bright, which is likewise invisible, though in a different way from darkness. Similarly hearing has to do with noise and silence, the former being audible, the latter inaudible, and, further, with loud noise, to which it is related as vision is to brightness, a loud and a violent sound being in a manner just as inaudible as a faint sound. The term invisible, be it noted, is applied not only to that which it is wholly impossible to see, which corresponds to other cases of the impossible, but also when a thing has imperfectly or not at all its natural properties, answering to the footless and the kernel-less. So, too, taste has for object not only that which can be tasted, but also the tasteless, by which we mean that which has little flavour or hardly any at all, or a flavour destructive of the taste. Now in flavour this distinction is supposed to start with the drinkable and the undrinkable. Both are tastes of a sort, but the latter is poor or destructive of the faculty of taste, while the former is naturally adapted to it. The drinkable is the common object of touch and of taste. But, since the object of taste is moist, the sense-organ which perceives it must be neither actually moist nor yet incapable of becoming moist. For taste is acted upon by the object of taste as such. The organ of taste, then, which needs to be moistened, must have the capacity of absorbing moisture without being dissolved, while at the same time it must not be actually moist. A proof of this is the fact that the tongue has no perception either when very dry or very moist. In the latter case the contact is with the moisture originally in the tongue, just as when a man first makes trial of a strong flavour and then tastes some other flavour; or as with the sick, to whom all things appear bitter because they perceive them with their tongue full of bitter moisture.

As with the colours, so with the species of flavour, there are, firstly, simple flavours, which are opposites, the sweet and the bitter; next to these on one side the succulent, on the other the salt; and, thirdly, intermediate between these, the pungent, the rough, the astringent and the acid. These seem to be practically all the varieties of flavour. Consequently, while the faculty of taste has potentially the qualities just described, the object of taste converts the potentiality into actuality.

Chapter 11

The same account is to be given of touch and the tangible. If touch is not a single sense but includes more senses than one, there must be a plurality of tangible objects also. It is a question whether touch is several senses or only one. What, moreover, is the sense-organ for the faculty of touch? Is it the flesh or what is analogous to this in creatures that have not flesh? Or is flesh, on the contrary, the medium, while the primary sense-organ is something different, something internal? We may argue thus: every sense seems to deal with a single pair of opposites, sight with white and black, hearing with high and low pitch, taste with bitter and sweet; but under the tangible are included several pairs of opposites, hot and cold, dry and moist, hard and soft and the like. A partial solution of this difficulty lies in the consideration that the other senses also apprehend more than one pair of opposites. Thus in vocal sound there is not only high and low pitch, but also loudness and faintness, smoothness and roughness, and so on. In regard to colour also there are other similar varieties. But what the one thing is which is subordinated to touch as sound is to hearing is not clear.

But is the organ of sense internal or is the flesh the immediate organ? No inference can be drawn, seemingly, from the fact that the sensation occurs simultaneously with contact. For even under present conditions, if a sort of membrane were constructed and stretched over the flesh, this would immediately on contact transmit the sensation as before. And yet it is clear that the organ of sense is not in this membrane; although, if by growth it became united to the flesh, the sensation would be transmitted even more quickly. Hence it appears that the part of the body in question, that is, the flesh, is related to us as the air would be if it were united to us all round by natural growth. We should then have thought we were perceiving sound, colour and smell by one and the same instrument: in fact, sight, hearing and smell would have seemed to us in a manner to constitute a single sense. But as it is, owing to the media, by which the various motions are transmitted, being separated from us, the difference of the organs of these three senses is manifest. But in regard to touch this point is at present obscure.

In fact, the animate body cannot consist of air or water singly, it must be something solid. The only alternative is that it should be a compound of earth and of these elements, as flesh and what is analogous to flesh profess to be. Consequently the body must be the naturally cohering medium for the faculty of touch, through which the plurality of sensations is communicated. That they are a plurality is made clear by touch in the case of the tongue, for the tongue perceives all tangible objects, and that at the same part at which it perceives flavour. Now, if the rest of the flesh also had perception of flavour, taste and touch would have seemed to be one and the same sense: whereas they are really two, because their organs are not interchangeable.

Here a question arises. All body has depth, this being the third dimension, and, if between two bodies a third body is interposed, the two cannot touch one another. Now that which is fluid is not independent of body, nor is that which is wet: if it is not itself water, it must contain water. But when bodies touch one another in the water, since their exterior surfaces are not dry, there must be water between them, the water with which their extremities are flooded. If, then, all this be true, no one thing can possibly touch another in the water, nor yet in the air: for the air stands to the objects in the air as water to the things in water, but this fact we are more apt to overlook, just as aquatic animals fail to notice that the things which touch one another in the water have wet surfaces. The question then arises: is the mode of perception uniform for all objects or does it differ for different objects? According to the prevalent view, taste and touch operate by direct contact, while the other senses operate at a distance. But this view is incorrect. On the contrary, we perceive the hard and the soft also mediately, just as much as we do the resonant, the visible, the odorous. But the latter are perceived at a distance, the former close at hand: and this is why the fact escapes us, since we really perceive all objects through a medium, though in touch and taste we fail to notice this. And yet, as we mentioned above, even if we perceived all objects of touch through a membrane without being aware of its interference, we should be just in the same position as we are now with regard to objects in the water or in the air: for, as it is, we suppose that we are touching the objects themselves and that there is no intervening medium. But there is this difference between the tangible on the one hand and visible and resonant things on the other: the latter we perceive because the medium acts in a certain way upon us, while tangible objects we perceive not by any action upon us of the medium, but concurrently with it, like the man who is struck through his shield. It is not that the shield was first struck and then passed on the blow, but, as it happened, both were struck simultaneously. And, generally, it would seem that the flesh and the tongue are related to the true sense-organ as are air and water to the organs of sight, hearing and smell respectively. But neither in the one case nor in the other would sensation follow on contact with the sense-organ; for instance, if a body that is white were placed on the outer surface of the eye: which shows that the instrument that apprehends the tangible is within. We should then get the same result as in the case of the other senses. What is placed on the sense-organ we do not perceive: what is placed on the flesh we do perceive: therefore flesh is the medium for the faculty of touch.

It is, then, the distinctive qualities of body as body which are the objects of touch: I mean those qualities which determine the elements, hot or cold, dry or moist, of which we have previously given an account in our discussion of the elements. And their sense-organ, the tactile organ, that is, in which the sense called touch primarily resides, is the part which has potentially the qualities of the tangible object. For perceiving is a sort of suffering or being acted upon: so that when the object makes the organ in actuality like itself it does so because that organ is potentially like it. Hence it is that we do not perceive what is just as hot or cold, hard or soft, as we are, but only the excesses of these qualities: which implies that the sense is a kind of mean between the opposite extremes in the sensibles. This is why it passes judgment on the things of sense. For the mean is capable of judging, becoming to each extreme in turn its opposite. And, as that which is to perceive white and black must not be actually either, though potentially both, and similarly for the other senses also, so in the case of touch the organ must be neither hot nor cold. Further, sight is in a manner, as we saw, of the invisible as well as the visible, and in same way the remaining senses deal with opposites. So, too, touch is of the tangible and the intangible: where by intangible is meant, first, that which has the distinguishing quality of things tangible in quite a faint degree, as is the case with the air; and, secondly, tangibles which are in excess, such as those which are positively destructive. Each of the senses, then, has now been described in outline.

Chapter 12

In regard to all sense generally we must understand that sense is that which is receptive of sensible forms apart from their matter, as wax receives the imprint of the signet-ring apart from the iron or gold of which it is made: it takes the imprint which is of gold or bronze, but not *quâ* gold or bronze. And similarly sense as relative to each sensible is acted upon by that which possesses colour, flavour or sound, not in so far as each of those sensibles is called a particular thing, but in so far as it possesses a particular quality and in respect of its character or form. The primary sense-organ is that in which such a power resides, the power to receive sensible forms. Thus the organ is one and the same with the power, but logically distinct from it. For that which perceives must be an extended magnitude. Sensitivity, however, is not an extended magnitude, nor is the sense: they are rather a certain character or power of the organ. From this it is evident why excesses in the sensible objects destroy the sense-organs. For if the motion is too violent for the sense-organ, the character or form (and this, as we saw, constitutes the sense) is annulled, just as the harmony and the pitch of the lyre suffer by too violent jangling of the strings. It is evident, again, why plants have no sensation, although they have one part of soul and are in some degree affected by the things themselves which are tangible: for example, they become cold and hot. The reason is that they have in them no mean, no principle capable of receiving the forms of sensible objects without their matter, but on the contrary, when they are acted upon, the matter acts upon them as well. It might be asked whether what is unable to smell would be in way acted upon by an odour, or that which is incapable of seeing by colour, and so for the other sensibles. But, if the object of smell is odour, the effect it produces, if it produces an effect at all, is smelling. Therefore none of the things that are unable to smell can be acted upon by odour, and the same is true of the other senses: nor can things be acted upon when they have the power of sensation, except as they individually possess the particular sense required. This may also be shown as follows. Light and darkness do not act upon bodies at all; neither does sound nor odour: it is the things which possess them that act. Thus it is the air accompanying the thunderbolt which rives the timber. But, it may be said, things tangible and flavours do so act: else by what agency are inanimate things acted upon or changed? Shall we, then, conclude that the objects of the other senses likewise act directly? Is it not rather the case that not all body can be affected by smell and sound, and that the bodies which are so affected are indeterminate and shifting; for example, air? For odour in the air implies that the air has been acted upon in some way. What then is smelling, besides a sort of suffering or being acted upon? Or shall we say that the act of smelling implies sense-perception, whereas the air, after it has been acted upon, so far from perceiving, at once becomes itself perceptible to sense?

BOOK III

Chapter 1

That there is no other sense distinct from the five, by which I mean sight, hearing, smell, taste, touch, anyone may convince himself on the following grounds. Let us assume that, as a matter of fact, we have sensation of every sensible object for which touch is the appropriate sense, all qualities of the tangible, as such, being perceptible to us through touch. Let us further assume that, when any sense is lacking to us, an organ of sense must also be lacking; and further, that whatever we perceive by actual contact is perceptible by touch, a sense which we do possess, while whatever we perceive mediately and not by actual contact is perceptible by means of the elements, namely, air and water. And here are implied two cases. Suppose, a first, we have perception by one and the same medium of two several things, different in kind from one another, then whoever possesses the appropriate sense-organ must be percipient of both: as, for example, if the sense-organ consists of air and air is also the medium of both sound and colour. Next suppose several media to transmit the same object, as both air and water transmit colour, both being transparent, then he who possesses one of these alone will perceive whatever is perceptible through both media. Now, of the elements, air and water are the only two of which sense-organs are composed. For the pupil of the eye is of water, and the ear is of air, and the organ of smell is of one or the other, while fire, if present anywhere, enters into all, since nothing can be sentient without warmth. Earth, again, belongs to none of the sense-organs, or, at most, is a constituent peculiar to touch. It follows, then, that outside water and air there is no sense-organ. Now sense-organs composed of air and water certain animals do, in fact, possess. We may infer, then, that all the senses are possessed by those animals which are fully developed and are not crippled: even the mole is found to have eyes beneath its skin. And thus, unless there exists some unknown body or some property different from any possessed by any of the bodies within our experience, there can be no sixth sense which we lack.

Nor, again, can there be any special sense-organ for the common sensibles, which we perceive incidentally by every sense; motion, rest, figure, magnitude, number, unity. For all of these we perceive by motion. Thus it is by motion that we perceive magnitude, and consequently figure, figure being one variety of magnitude; while that which is at rest we perceive by the fact that it is not moved. Number we perceive by the negation of continuity and by the special sense-organs also: for each sensation has a single object. Clearly, then, it is impossible that there should be a special sense for any one of these; for example, motion: for in that case we should perceive them in the same way as we now perceive sweetness by sight (and this we do because we have a sense which perceives both, and by this we actually apprehend the two simultaneously when they occur in conjunction). Otherwise we should never have more than an incidental perception of them; as of Cleon's son we perceive not that he is Cleon's son, but that he is a white object, and the fact of his being Cleon's son is accessory to the whiteness. But of the common sensibles we have already a common perception, which is direct and not indirect, so that there cannot be a special sense for them. For, if there were, we should never perceive them otherwise than in the way in which we said we saw Cleon's son.

But the various senses incidentally perceive each other's proper objects, not as so many separate senses, but as forming a single sense, when there is concurrent perception relating to the same object; as, for instance, when we perceive that gall is bitter and yellow. For it is certainly not the part of any other sense to declare that both objects are one and the same. Hence you are sometimes deceived and, on observing something yellow, fancy it to be gall.

But, it might be asked, why have we several senses, instead of only one? I answer, it is in order that we may not be so likely to overlook the common attributes, such as motion, magnitude, number, which accompany the special sensibles. For, if sight had been our only sense and whiteness its object, we should have been more apt to overlook the common sensibles and to confuse all sensibles, because colour and magnitude, for instance, must always go together. As it is, the fact that the common attributes are found in the object of another sense also shows that they are severally distinct.

Chapter 2

Inasmuch as we perceive that we see and hear, it must either be by sight or by some other sense that the percipient perceives that he sees. But, it may be urged, the same sense which perceives sight will also perceive the colour which is the object of sight. So that either there will be two senses to perceive the same thing or the one sense, sight, will perceive itself. Further, if the sense perceiving sight were really a distinct sense, either the series would go on to infinity or some one of the series of senses would perceive itself. Therefore it will be better to admit this of the first in the series. Here, however, there is a difficulty. Assuming that to perceive by sight is to see and that it is colour or that which possesses colour which is seen, it may be argued that, if you are to see that which sees, that which in the first instance sees, the primary visual organ, will actually have colour. Clearly, then, to perceive by sight does not always mean one and the same thing. For, even when we do not see, it is nevertheless by sight that we discern both darkness and light, though not in the same manner. Further, that which sees is in a manner coloured. For the sense-organ is in every case receptive of the sensible object without its matter. And this is why the sensations and images remain in the sense-organs even when the sensible objects are withdrawn.

Now the actuality of the sensible object is one and the same with that of the sense, though, taken in the abstract, sensible object and sense are not the same. I mean, for example, actual sound and actual hearing are the same: for it is possible to have hearing and yet not hear; again, that which is resonant is not always sounding. But when that which is capable of hearing operantly hears and that which is capable of sounding sounds, the actual hearing and the actual sound occur simultaneously, and we might, if we pleased, call them audition and resonance respectively. If, then, motion, action and passivity reside in that which is acted upon, then of necessity it is in the potentiality of hearing that there is actual sound and there is actual hearing. For the activity of agent and movent comes into play in the patient; and this is why that which causes motion need not itself be moved. The actuality of the resonant, then, is sound or resonance, and the actuality of that which can hear is hearing or audition, hearing and sound both having two meanings. The same account may be given of the other senses and their objects. For, just as acting and being acted upon are in the subject acted upon and not in the agent, so also the actuality of the sensible object and that of the sensitive faculty will be in the percipient subject. But in some cases both activities have a name; for example, resonance and audition: in other cases one or the other has no name. Thus, while the actuality of sight is called seeing, that of colour has no name; and, while the actuality of the taste-faculty is called tasting, that of the flavour has no name.

Now, as the actuality of the object and that of the faculty of sense are one and the same, although taken in the abstract they are different, hearing and sound thus understood as operant must simultaneously cease to be or simultaneously continue in being, and so also with flavour and taste, and similarly with the other senses and their objects: but when they are understood as potentialities, there is no such necessity. On this point the earlier natural philosophers were in error when they supposed that without seeing there was neither white nor black, and without tasting no flavour. Their statement is in one sense true, in another false. For the terms sensation and sensible thing are ambiguous. When they mean the actual sensation and the actual sensible thing, the statement holds good: when they mean potential sensation and potential sensible, this is not the case. But our predecessors used terms without distinguishing their various meanings.

If, then, concord consists in a species of vocal sound, and if vocal sound and hearing are in one aspect one and the same, (though in another aspect not the same) and if concord is a proportion, it follows that hearing must also be a species of proportion. And this is the reason why hearing is destroyed by either excess, whether of high pitch or of low. And similarly, in the case of flavours, excess destroys the taste, and in colours excessive brightness or darkness destroys the sight, and so with smell, whether the excessive odour be agreeable or pungent. All this implies that the sense is a proportion. Hence sensibles are, it is true, pleasurable when they are brought into the range of this proportion pure and unmixed; for example, the shrill, the sweet, the salt: in that case, I say, they are pleasurable. But, speaking generally, that in which ingredients are blended is pleasurable in a higher degree, accord more pleasurable to the ear than high pitch or low pitch alone, and to touch that which admits of being still further heated or cooled. The due proportion constitutes the sense, while objects in excess give pain or cause destruction.

Now each sense is concerned with its own sensible object, being resident in the organ, *quâ* sense-organ, and judges the specific differences of its own sensible object. Thus sight pronounces upon white and black, taste upon sweet and bitter, and so with the rest. But, since we compare white and sweet and each of the sensibles with each, what in fact is it by means of which we perceive the difference between them? It must be by sense, for they are sensibles. And thus it is clear that the flesh is not the ultimate organ of sense; for, if it were, it would be necessary that that which judges should judge by contact with the sensible object. Nor indeed can we with separate organs judge that sweet is different from white, but both objects must be clearly presented to some single faculty. For, if we could, then the mere fact of my perceiving one thing and your perceiving another would make it clear that the two things were different. But the single faculty is required to pronounce them different, for sweet and white are pronounced to be different. It is one and the same faculty, then, which so pronounces. Hence, as it pronounces, so it also thinks and perceives. Clearly, then, it is not possible with separate organs to pronounce judgment upon things which are separate: nor yet at separate times, as the following considerations show. For, as it is one single faculty which pronounces that good and bad are different, so when it judges "A is different from B" it also judges "B is different from A" (and in this case the "when" is not accidental; I mean, accidental in the sense in which I may now say "Such and such things are different" without saying that they are different now. On the contrary, it pronounces now and pronounces that A and B are different now). That which judges judges, then, instantaneously and hence as an inseparable unit in an inseparable time. But, again, it is impossible for the same thing, in so far as indivisible and affected in indivisible time, to be moved at the same instant with contrary motions. For, if the object be sweet, it moves sense or thought in such and such a way, but what is bitter moves it in a contrary way, and what is white in a different way. Is then, that which judges instantaneous in its judgment and numerically undivided and inseparable, although separated logically? Then it is in a certain sense that which is divided which perceives divided objects; in another sense it is *quâ* indivisible that the divided perceives them: that is to say, logically it is divisible, locally and numerically it is indivisible. Or is this impossible? For the same indivisible unity, though in potentiality each of two opposites, in the order of thought and being is not so, but in actual operation is divided: it is impossible that it should be at the same time both white and black, and hence impossible that it should receive at the same time the forms of white and black, if reception of the forms constitutes sensation and thought. Rather is the case parallel to that of the point, as some describe it, which is divisible in so far as it is regarded as one or two. Well then, in so far as the faculty which judges is indivisible, it is one and judges instantaneously; but, in so far as it is divisible, it is not one, for it uses the same point at the same time twice. So far as it treats the boundary-point as two, it passes judgment on two separate things with a faculty which in a manner is separated into two; so far as it treats the point as one, it passes judgment on one thing, and that instantaneously. So much, then, for the principle in virtue of which we call the animal capable of sensation.

Chapter 3

There are two different characteristics by which the soul is principally defined firstly, motion from place to place and, secondly, thinking and judging and perceiving. Both thought and intelligence are commonly regarded as a kind of perception, since the soul in both of these judges and recognises something existent. The ancients, at any rate, identify intelligence and perception: thus, in the words of Empedocles: "Wisdom for mankind is increased according to that which is present to them": and again "Whence they have also continually a shifting succession of thoughts." Homer's meaning, too, is the same when he says: "Such is the mind of men." In fact, all of them conceive thought to be corporeal like sensation and hold that we understand, as well as perceive, like by like: as we explained at the outset of the discussion.

Now it is clear that perception and intelligence are not the same thing. For all animals share in the one, but only a few in the other. And when we come to thinking, which includes right thinking and wrong thinking, right thinking being intelligence, knowledge and true opinion, and wrong thinking the opposites of these, neither is this identical with perception. For perception of the objects of the special senses is always true and is found in all animals, while thinking may be false as well as true and is found in none which have not reason also. Imagination, in fact, is something different both from perception and from thought, and is never found by itself apart from perception, any more than is belief apart from imagination. Clearly thinking is not the same thing as believing. For the former is in our own power, whenever we please: for we can represent an object before our eyes, as do those who range things under mnemonic headings and picture them to themselves. But opining is not in our power, for the opinion that we hold must be either false or true. Moreover, when we are of opinion that something is terrible or alarming, we at once feel the corresponding emotion, and so, too, with what is reassuring. But when we are under the influence of imagination we are no more affected than if we saw in a picture the objects which inspire terror or confidence. There are also different forms even of belief: knowledge, opinion, intelligence and their opposites. But the difference between these species must be reserved for another discussion.

To turn to thought: since it is different from sense-perception and seems to include imagination on the one hand and conception on the other, we must determine the nature of imagination before we proceed to discuss conception. If, then, imagination is the faculty in virtue of which we say that an image presents itself to us, and if we exclude the metaphorical use of the term, it is some one of the faculties or habits in virtue of which we judge, and judge truly or falsely. Such faculties or habits are sensation, opinion, knowledge, intellect. It is clearly not sensation, for the following reasons. Sensation is either a faculty like sight or an activity like seeing. But we may have an image even when neither the one nor the other is present: for example, the images in dreams. Again, sensation is always present, but not so imagination. Besides, the identity of the two in actuality would involve the possibility that all the brutes have imagination. But this apparently is not the case; for example, the ant, the bee and the grub do not possess it. Moreover, sensations are always true, but imaginings prove for the most part false. Further, it is not when we direct our energies closely to the sensible object, that we say that this object appears to us to be a man, but rather when we do not distinctly perceive it (then the term true or false is applied). And, as we said before, visions present themselves even if we have our eyes closed.

Neither, again, can imagination be ranked with the faculties, like knowledge or intellect, which always judge truly: it may also be false. It remains, then, to consider whether it be opinion, as opinion may be true or false. But opinion is attended by conviction, for it is impossible to hold opinions without being convinced of them: but no brute is ever convinced, though many have imagination. Further, every opinion implies conviction, conviction implies that we have been persuaded, and persuasion implies reason. Among brutes, however, though some have imagination, none have reason. It is evident, then, that imagination is neither opinion joined with sensation nor opinion through sensation, nor yet a complex of opinion and sensation, both on these grounds and because nothing else is the object of opinion but that which is the object of sensation: I mean, it is the complex of the opinion of white and the sensation of white, not surely of the opinion of good with the sensation of white, which alone could constitute imagination. To imagine, then, will be on this supposition to opine directly, not indirectly, that which we perceive. But there are false imaginings concerning things of which we hold at the same time a true conception. For example, the sun appears only a foot in diameter, but we are convinced that it is larger than the inhabited world: in this case, therefore, either, without any alteration in the thing and without any lapse of memory on our part or conversion by argument, we have abandoned the true opinion which we had about it; or else, if we still retain it, the same opinion must be both true and false. It could have proved false only in the event of the object having changed without our observing it. It is not, then, either one of the two, opinion and sensation, singly, or a combination of the two, which constitutes imagination.

Now when one thing is moved, something else can be moved by it. And imagination is thought to be a species of motion and not to arise apart from sensation, but only in sentient beings and with the objects of sense for its objects. Motion, again, may it is a produced by actual sensation, and such motion must resemble the sensation which caused it. From all this it follows that this particular motion cannot arise apart from sensation nor be found anywhere except in sentient beings: and in virtue of this motion it is possible for its possessor to do and experience many things: imagination, too, may be both true and false. The reasons for the last conclusion are as follows. Perception   of the objects of the special senses is true, or subject to the minimum of error. Next comes the perception that they are attributes: and at this point error may come in. As to the whiteness of an object sense is never mistaken, but it may be mistaken as to whether the white object is this thing or something else. Thirdly, there is perception of the common attributes, that is, the concomitants of the things to which the special attributes belong: I mean, for example, motion and magnitude, which are attributes of sensibles. And it is concerning them that sense is most apt to be deceived. But the motion which is the result of actual sensation will be different according as it arises from one or other of these three kinds of perception. The first kind, so long as the sensation is present, is true: the other kinds may be false, whether the sensation is present or absent, and especially when the object perceived is a long way off. If then, imagination possesses no other characteristics than the aforesaid, and if it is what it has been described to be, imagination will be a motion generated by actual perception. And, since sight is the principal sense, imagination has derived even its name (φαντασία) from light (φάος), because without light one cannot see. Again, because imaginations remain in us and resemble the corresponding sensations, animals perform many actions under their influence; some, that is, the brutes, through not having intellect, and others, that is, men, because intellect is sometimes obscured by passion or disease or sleep. Let this account of the nature and cause of imagination suffice.

Chapter 4

As to the part of the soul with which it knows and understands, whether such part be separable spatially, or not separable spatially, but only in thought, we have to consider what is its distinctive character and how thinking comes about. Now, if thinking is analogous to perceiving, it will consist in a being acted upon by the object of thought or in something else of this kind. This part of the soul, then, must be impassive, but receptive of the form and potentially like this form, though not identical with it: and, as the faculty of sense is to sensible objects, so must intellect be related to intelligible objects. The mind, then, since it thinks all things, must needs, in the words of Anaxagoras, be unmixed with any, if it is to rule, that is, to know. For by intruding its own form it hinders and obstructs that which is alien to it; hence it has no other nature than this, that it is a capacity. Thus, then, the part of the soul which we call intellect (and by intellect I mean that whereby the soul thinks and conceives) is nothing at all actually before it thinks. Hence, too, we cannot reasonably conceive it to be mixed with the body: for in that case it would acquire some particular quality, cold or heat, or would even have some organ, as the perceptive faculty has. But as a matter of fact it has none. Therefore it has been well said that the soul is a place of forms or ideas: except that this is not true of the whole soul, but only of the soul which can think, and again that the forms are there not in actuality, but potentially. But that the impassivity of sense is different from 5 that of intellect is clear if we look at the sense-organs and at sense. The sense loses its power to perceive, if the sensible object has been too intense: thus it cannot hear sound after very loud noises, and after too powerful colours and odours it can neither see nor smell. But the intellect, when it has been thinking on an object of intense thought, is not less, but even more, able to think of inferior objects. For the perceptive faculty is not independent of body, whereas intellect is separable. But when the intellect has thus become everything in the sense in which one who actually is a scholar is said to be so (which happens so soon as he can exercise his power of himself), even then it is still in one sense but a capacity: not, however, a capacity in the same sense as before it learned or discovered. And, moreover, at this stage intellect is capable of thinking itself.

Now, since magnitude is not the same as the quiddity of magnitude, nor water the same as the quiddity of water form or (and so also of many other things, though not of all, the thing and its quiddity being in some cases the same), we judge the quiddity of flesh and flesh itself either with different instruments or with the same instrument in different relations. For flesh is never found apart from matter, but, like "snub-nosed", it is a particular form in a particular matter. It is, then, with the faculty of sense that we discriminate heat and cold and all those qualities of which flesh is a certain proportion. But it is with another faculty, either separate from sense, or related to it as the bent line when it is straightened out is related to its former self, that we discriminate the quiddity of flesh. Again, when we come to the abstractions of mathematics, the straight answers to the quality "snub-nosed", being never found apart from extension. But the straightness of that which is straight, always supposing that the straight is not the same as straightness, is something distinct: we may, for instance, assume the definition of straightness to be duality. It is, then, with another instrument or with the same instrument in another relation that we judge it. In general, therefore, to the separation of the things from their matter corresponds a difference in the operations of the intellect.

The question might arise: assuming that the mind is something simple and impassive and, in the words of Anaxagoras, has nothing in common with anything else, how will it think, if to think is to be acted upon? For it is in so far as two things have something in common that the one of them is supposed to act and the other to be acted upon. Again, can mind itself be its own object? For then either its other objects will have mind in them, if it is not through something else, but in itself, that mind is capable of being thought, and if to be so capable is everywhere specifically one and the same; or else the mind will have, some ingredient in its composition which makes it, like the rest, an object of thought. Or shall we recall our old distinction between two meanings of the phrase "to be acted upon in virtue of a common element," and say that the mind is in a manner potentially all objects of thought, but is actually none of them until it thinks: potentially in the same sense as in a tablet which has nothing actually written upon it the writing exists potentially? This is exactly the case with the mind. Moreover, the mind itself is included among the objects which can be thought. For where the objects are immaterial that which thinks and that which is thought are identical. Speculative knowledge and its object are identical. (We must, however, enquire why we do not think always.) On the other hand, in things containing matter each of the objects of thought is present potentially. Consequently material objects will not have mind in them, for the mind is the power of becoming such objects without their matter; whereas the mind will have the attribute of being its own object.

Chapter 5

But since, as in the whole of nature, to something which serves as matter for each kind (and this is potentially all the members of the kind) there corresponds something else which is the cause or agent because it makes them all, the two being related to one another as art to its material, of necessity these differences must be found also in the soul. And to the one intellect, which answers to this description because it becomes all things, corresponds the other because it makes all things, like a sort of definite quality such as light. For in a manner light, too, converts colours which are potential into actual colours. And it is this intellect which is separable and impassive and unmixed, being in its essential nature an activity. For that which acts is always superior to that which is acted upon, the cause or principle to the matter. Now actual knowledge is identical with the thing known, but potential knowledge is prior in time in the individual; and yet not universally prior in time. But this intellect has no intermittence in its thought. It is, however, only when separated that it is its true self, and this, its essential nature, alone is immortal and eternal. But we do not remember because this is impassive, while the intellect which can be affected is perishable and without this does not think at all.

Chapter 6

The process of thinking indivisible wholes belongs to a sphere from which falsehood is excluded. But where both truth and falsehood are possible there is already some combining of notions into one. As, in the words of Empedocles, "where sprang into being the neckless heads of many creatures," then afterwards Love put them together, so these notions, first separate, are combined; as, for instance, the notions incommensurable and diagonal. And, if the thinking refers to the past or to the future, the notion of time is included in the combination. Falsehood, in fact, never arises except when notions are combined. For, even if white be asserted to be not-white, not-white is brought into a combination. We may equally well call every statement a disjunction. But at any rate under truth and falsehood we include not only the assertion that Cleon is white, but also the assertion that he was or will be. And the unifying principle is in every case the mind.

Since, however, the term indivisible has two meanings, according as a whole is not potentially divisible or is actually undivided, there is nothing to hinder us from thinking an indivisible whole, when we think of a length (that being actually undivided), or from thinking it in an indivisible time. For the time is a divisible or indivisible unit in the same way as the length thought of. We cannot therefore state what the mind thinks in each half of the time. For, if the whole be undivided, the half has only potential existence. But, if the mind thinks each half separately, it simultaneously divides the time also. And in that case it is as if the parts were separate lengths. If, however, the mind conceives the length as made up of the two halves, then the time may be regarded as made up of corresponding halves.

Again, that which is not quantitatively but specifically an indivisible whole the mind thinks in an indivisible unit of time and by an indivisible mental act. *Per accidens* however, such specific unity is divisible, though not in the same way as they, the act of thought and the time required for the act, are divisible, but in the same way as they are whole and indivisible. For in these specific unities also there is present a something indivisible, though certainly not separately existent, the same as that which constitutes the unity of both the time and the length. And, as with time and length, so in like manner with whatever is continuous. But the point and every division and whatever is an undivided whole in the same sense as the point is clearly explained by the analogy of privation. And the same explanation holds in all other cases. How, for instance, is evil apprehended, or black? In some fashion by its contrary. But that which apprehends must potentially be, and must contain within itself, the contrary which it apprehends. If, however, there be something which has no contrary (*some one of the causes*), then it is itself the content of its own knowledge, is in actuality and is separately existent.

Now every proposition, like an affirmative proposition, predicating something of something, is true or false. But with thought this is not always so. When its object is the What in the sense of the quiddity and there is no predication, thought is in every case true. But, as the perception by sight of the proper object of sight is infallibly true, whereas in the question whether the white object is a man or not, perception by sight is not always true, so is it with immaterial objects.

Chapter 7

Now actual knowledge is identical with the thing known. But potential knowledge is prior in time in the individual, and yet not universally prior even in time. For it is from something actually existent that all which comes into being is derived. And manifestly the sensible object simply brings the faculty of sense which was potential into active exercise: in this transition, in fact, the sense is not acted upon or qualitatively changed. Consequently this must be a different species of motion. For motion is, as we saw, an activity of that which is imperfect; but activity in the absolute sense, that is, activity of that which has reached perfection, is quite distinct.

Sensation, then, is analogous to simple assertion or simple apprehension by thought and, when the sensible thing is pleasant or painful, the pursuit or avoidance of it by the soul is a sort of affirmation or negation. In fact, to feel pleasure or pain is precisely to function with the sensitive mean, acting upon good or evil as such. It is in this that actual avoidance and actual appetition consist: nor is the appetitive faculty distinct from the faculty of avoidance, nor either from the sensitive faculty; though logically they are different. But to the thinking soul images serve as present sensations: and when it affirms or denies good or evil, it avoids or pursues (this is why the soul never thinks without an image). To give an illustration: the air impresses a certain quality on the pupil of the eye, and this in turn upon something else, and so also with the organ of hearing, while the last thing to be impressed is one and is a single mean, though with a plurality of distinct aspects.

What that is by which the soul judges that sweet is different from warm has been explained above, but must be restated here. It is a unity, but one in the same sense as a boundary point, and its object, the unity by analogy of these two sensibles or their numerical unity, is related to each of the two in turn as they, taken separately, are to each other. For what difference does it make whether we ask how we judge the sensibles that do not fall under the same genus, or the contraries which do, like white and black? Suppose, then, that as A, the white, is to B, the black, so C is to D (that is, as those sensibles are to one another). It follows, convertendo, that A is to C as B to D. If, then, C and D are attributes of a single subject, the relation between them, like that between A and B, will be that they are one and the same, though the aspects they present are distinct: and so, too, of their single subject. The same would hold, supposing A were the sweet and B the white.

Thus it is the forms which the faculty of thought thinks in mental images. And, as in the region of sense the objects of pursuit and avoidance have been defined for it, so also outside sensation, when engaged with images, it is moved to action: as, for instance, you perceive a beacon and say "That is fire"; and then (by the central sense), seeing it in motion, you recognise that it signals the approach of an enemy. But at other times under the influence of the images or thoughts in the soul you calculate as though you had the objects before your eyes and deliberate about the future in the light of the present. And when you pronounce, just as there in sensation you affirm the pleasant or the painful, here in thought you pursue or avoid: and so in action generally. And, further, what is unrelated to action, as truth and falsehood, is in the same class with the good and the evil. Yet in this, at any rate, they differ, that the former are absolute, the latter relative to some one concerned.

But the abstractions of mathematics, as they are called, the mind thinks as it might conceive the snub-nosed; *quâ* snub-nosed, it would not be conceived apart from flesh, whereas *quâ* hollow, if anyone ever had actually so conceived it, he would have conceived it without the flesh in which the hollowness resides. So, too, when we think of mathematical objects, we conceive them though not in fact separate from matter, as though they were separate. And, speaking generally, mind in active operation is its objects (when it thinks them). The question, whether it is possible for the mind to think anything which is unextended without being itself unextended, must for the present be postponed.

Chapter 8

And now let us sum up what has been said concerning the soul by repeating that in a manner the soul is all existent things. For they are all either objects of sensation or objects of thought; and knowledge and sensation are in a manner identical with their respective objects. How this is so requires to be explained. Knowledge and sensation, then, are subdivided to correspond to the things. Potential knowledge and sensation answer to things which are potential, actual knowledge and sensation to things which are actual, while the sensitive and the cognitive faculties in the soul are potentially these objects; I mean, object of sensation and object of cognition respectively. It follows that the faculties must be identical, if not with the things themselves, then with their forms. The things themselves they are not, for it is not the stone which is in the soul, but the form of the stone. So that there is an analogy between the soul and the hand; for, as the hand is the instrument of instruments, so the intellect is the form of forms and sensation the form of sensibles. But, since apart from sensible magnitudes there is nothing, as it would seem, independently existent, it is in the sensible forms that the intelligible forms exist, both the abstractions of mathematics, as they are called, and all the qualities and attributes of sensible things. And for this reason, as without sensation a man would not learn or understand anything, so at the very time when he is actually thinking he must have an image before him. For mental images are like present sensations, except that they are immaterial. Imagination, however, is distinct from affirmation and negation, for it needs a combination of notions to constitute truth or falsehood. But, it may be asked, how will the simplest notions differ in character from mental images? I reply that neither these nor the rest of our notions are images, but that they cannot dispense with images.

Chapter 9

The soul in animals has been defined in virtue of two faculties, not only by its capacity to judge, which is the function of thought and perception, but also by the local movement which it imparts to the animal. Assuming the nature of sensation and intellect to have been so far determined, we have now to consider what it is in the soul which initiates motion: whether it is some one part of the soul, which is either locally separable or logically distinct, or whether it is the whole soul: and again, if a separate part, whether it is a special part distinct from those usually recognised and from those enumerated above, or whether it coincides with some one of these. A question at once arises in what sense it is proper to speak of parts of the soul and how many there are. For in one sense there appear to be an infinite number of parts and not merely those which some distinguish, the reasoning, passionate and concupiscent parts, for which others substitute the rational and the irrational. For, if we examine the differences on which they base their divisions, we shall find that there are other parts separated by a greater distance than these; namely, the parts which we have just discussed, the nutritive, which belongs to plants as well as to all animals, and the sensitive, which cannot easily be either as rational or irrational. Imagination, again, is logically distinct from them all, while it is very difficult to say with which of the parts it is in fact identical or not identical, if we are to assume separate parts in the soul. Then besides these there is appetency, which would seem to be distinct both in concept and in capacity from all the foregoing. And surely it is absurd to split this up. For wish in the rational part corresponds to concupiscence and passion in the irrational. And, if we make a triple division of soul, there will be appetency in all three parts.

To come now to the question at present before us, what is it that imparts to the animal local movement? For as for the motion of growth and decay, which is found in all animals, it would seem that this must be originated by that part of soul which is found in all of them, the generative and nutritive part. Inspiration and expiration of breath, sleep and waking, subjects full of difficulty, call for subsequent enquiry. But to return to locomotion, we must enquire what it is that imparts to the animal progressive motion. That it is not the nutritive faculty is clear. For this motion is always directed to an end and is attended either by imagination or by appetency. No animal, which is not either seeking or avoiding something, moves except under compulsion. Moreover, if it were the nutritive faculty, plants also would be capable of locomotion and thus would have some part instrumental in producing this form of motion. Similarly it is not the sensitive faculty, since there are many animals which have sensation and yet are throughout their lives stationary and motionless. If, then, nature does nothing in vain and, except in mutilated and imperfect specimens, omits nothing that is indispensable, while the animals we are considering are fully developed and not mutilated - as is shown by the fact that they propagate their kind and have a period of maturity and a period of decline, it follows that, if locomotion was implied in sensation, they would have had the parts instrumental to progression. Nor, again, is it the reasoning faculty or what is called intellect that is the cause of motion. For the speculative intellect thinks nothing that is practical and makes no assertion about what is to be avoided or pursued, whereas motion always implies that we are avoiding or pursuing something. But, even if the mind has something of the kind before it, it does not forthwith prompt avoidance or pursuit. For example, it often thinks of something alarming or pleasant without prompting to fear; the only effect is a beating of the heart or, when the thought is pleasant, some other bodily movement. Besides, even if the intellect issues the order and the understanding bids us avoid or pursue something, still we are not thereby moved to act: on the contrary, action is determined by desire; in the case, for instance, of the incontinent man. And generally we see that, although a man possesses a knowledge of medicine, it does not follow that he practises; and this implies that there is something else apart from the knowledge which determines action in accordance with the knowledge. Nor, again, is it solely appetency on which this motion depends. The continent, though they feel desire, that is appetite, do not act as their desires prompt, but on the contrary obey reason.

Chapter 10

The motive causes are apparently, at any rate, these two, either appetency or intelligence, if we regard imagination as one species of thinking. For men often act contrary to knowledge in obedience to their imaginings, while in the other animals there is no process of thinking or reasoning, but solely imagination. Both these, then, are causes of locomotion, intelligence and appetency. By intelligence we mean that which calculates the means to an end, that is, the practical intellect, which differs from the speculative intellect by the end at which it aims. Appetency, too, is directed to some end in every case: for that which is the end of desire is the starting point of the practical intellect, and the last stage in this process of thought is the starting point of action. Hence there is good reason for the view that these two are the causes of motion, appetency and practical thought. For it is the object of appetency which causes motion; and the reason why thought causes motion is that the object of appetency is the starting point of thought. Again, when imagination moves to action, it does not move to action apart from appetency. Thus there is one single moving cause, the appetitive faculty. For, had there been two, intelligence and appetency, which moved to action, still they would have done so in virtue of some character common to both. But, as a matter of fact, intellect is not found to cause motion apart from appetency. For rational wish is appetency; and, when anyone is moved in accordance with reason, he is also moved according to rational wish. But appetency may move a man in opposition to reason, for concupiscence is a species of appetency. While, however, intellect is always right, appetency and imagination may be right or wrong. Hence it is invariably the object of appetency which causes motion, but this object may be either the good or the apparent good. Not all good, however, but practical good: where by practical good we mean something which may not be good under all circumstances.

It is evident, then, that motion is due to the faculty of the soul corresponding to this object - I mean what is known as appetency. But those who divide the soul into parts, if they divide it according to its powers and separate these from one another, will find that such parts tend to become very numerous: nutritive, sensitive, intelligent, deliberative, with the further addition of an appetent part: for these differ more widely from one another than the concupiscent does from the passionate. Now desires arise which are contrary to one another, and this occurs whenever reason and the appetites are opposed, that is, in those animals which have a perception of time. For intelligence bids us resist because of the future, while appetite has regard only to the immediate present; for the pleasure of the moment appears absolutely pleasurable and absolutely good because we do not see the future. Therefore, while generically the moving cause will be one, namely, the faculty of appetency, as such, and ultimately the object of appetency (which, without being in motion itself, causes motion by the mere fact of being thought of or imagined), numerically there is a plurality of moving causes.

Now motion implies three things, first, that which causes motion, secondly, that whereby it causes motion, and again, thirdly, that which is moved; and of these that which causes motion is twofold, firstly, that which is itself unmoved and, secondly, that which both causes motion and is itself moved. The unmoved movent is the practical good, that which is moved and causes motion is the appetitive faculty (for the animal which is moved is moved in so far as it desires, and desire is a species of motion or activity) and, finally, the thing moved is the animal. But the instrument with which desire moves it, once reached, is a part of the body: hence it must be dealt with under the functions common to body and soul. For the present, it may be enough to say summarily that we find that which causes motion by means of organs at the point where beginning and end coincide; as, for instance, they do in the hinge-joint, for there the convex and the concave are respectively the end and the beginning, with the result that the latter is at rest, while the former moves, convex and concave being logically distinct, but locally inseparable. For all animals move by pushing and pulling, and accordingly there must be in them a fixed point, like the centre in a circle, and from this the motion must begin. Thus, then, in general terms, as already stated, the animal is capable of moving itself just in so far as it is appetitive: and it cannot be appetitive without imagination. Now imagination may be rational or it may be imagination of sense. Of the latter the other animals also have a share.

Chapter 11

We must also consider what is the moving cause in those imperfect animals which have only the sense of touch. Is possible that they should have imagination and desire, or is it not? It is evident that they feel pleasure and pain: and, if they have these, then of necessity they must also feel desire. But how can they have imagination? Shall we say that, as their movements are vague and indeterminate, so, though they have these faculties, they have them in a vague and indeterminate form? The imagination of sense, then, as we have said, is found in the other animals also, but deliberative imagination in those alone which have reason. For the task of deciding whether to do this or that already implies reasoning. And the pursuit of the greater good necessarily implies some single standard of measurement. Hence we have the power of constructing a single image out of a number of images. And the reason why the lower animals are thought not to have opinion is that they do not possess that form of imagination which comes from inference, while the latter implies the former. And so appetency does not imply the deliberative faculty. But sometimes it overpowers rational wish and moves to action; at other times the latter, rational wish, overpowers the former, appetency. Thus one appetency prevails over another appetency, like one sphere over another sphere, in the case where incontinence has supervened. But by nature the upper sphere always has the predominance and is a moving cause, so that the motion is actually the resultant of three orbits.

The cognitive faculty, however, is not subject to motion, but is at rest. The major premiss is universal, whether judgment or proposition, while the minor has to do with a particular fact: for, while the former asserts that such and such a person ought to do such and such an act, the latter asserts that a particular act is one of the sort and that I am such a person. Now it is the latter judgment which at once moves to action, not the universal. Or shall we say that it is both together, but the one is akin to the unmoved movent, the other is not?

Chapter 12

Every living thing, then, must have the nutritive soul and in fact has a soul from its birth till its death. For what has been born must necessarily grow, reach maturity and decline, and for these processes nutriment is indispensable. It follows, then, of necessity that the nutritive faculty is present in all things that grow and decay. But sensation is not necessarily present in all living things. For wherever the body is uncompounded there can be no sense of touch (yet without this sense animal existence is impossible): nor, again, in those living things which are incapable of receiving forms apart from matter. But the animal must of necessity possess sensation, if nature necessary makes nothing in vain: for everything in nature subserves an end or else will be an accessory of things which subserve an end. Now every living body having the power of progression and yet lacking sensation would be destroyed and never reach full development, which is its natural function. For how in such a case is it to obtain nutriment? Motionless animals, it is true, have for nutriment that from which they have been developed. But a body, not stationary, but produced by generation, cannot possibly have a soul and an intelligence capable of judging without also having sensation. (Neither can it, if it be not generated.) For why should it have the one without the other? Presumably for the advantage either of the soul or of the body. But neither of these alternatives is, in fact, admissible. For the soul will be no better able to think, and the body will be no better off, for the absence of sensation. We conclude, then, that nobody that is not stationary has soul without having sensation.

But, further, the body, assuming that it has sensation, must be either simple or composite. But it cannot be simple, necessary for then it would not have touch, and this sense is indispensable. This is clear from the following considerations. The animal is an animate body. Now body is always tangible and it is that which is perceptible by touch which is tangible: from which it follows that the body of the animal must have tactile sensation, if the animal is to survive. For the other senses, that is to say, smell, sight, hearing, have media of sensation, but a being which has no sensation will be unable when it comes into contact with things to avoid some and seize others. And if this is so, it will be impossible for the animal to survive. This is why taste is a kind of touch, for taste is of nutriment and nutriment is body which is tangible; whereas sound, colour and smell afford no nourishment and promote neither growth nor decay. So that taste also must be a kind of touch, because it is a sensation of that which is tangible and nutritive. These two senses, then, are necessary to the animal, and it is plain that without touch no animal can exist.

But the other senses are means to well-being, and are necessary, not to any and every species of animal, but only to certain species, as, for example, those capable of locomotion. For, if the animal capable of locomotion is to survive, it must have sensation, not only when in contact with anything, but also at a distance from it. And this will be secured if it can perceive through a medium, the medium being capable of being acted upon and set in motion by the sensible object, and the animal itself by the medium. Now that which causes motion from place to place produces a change operating within certain limits, and that which propels causes the thing propelled to propel in turn, the movement being transmitted through something intermediate. The first in the series initiates motion and propels without being itself propelled, while the last is simply propelled without propelling; the numerous middle terms of the series both propel and are propelled. So it is also with qualitative change, except that what is subject to this change remains in the same place. Suppose we were to dip something into wax, the movement in the wax would extend just so far down as we had dipped the object, whereas in the like case a stone is not moved at all, while water is disturbed to a great distance and air is disturbed to the farthest extent possible and acts and is acted upon as long as it remains unbroken. And, to revert to the reflection of light, that is why, instead of holding that the visual ray leaving the eye is reflected, it would be better to say that the air is acted upon by the shape and colour, so long as it is one and unbroken. This is the case over any smooth surface: and accordingly the air acts on the organ of sight in turn, just as if the impress on the wax had penetrated right through to the other side.

Chapter 13

It is evident that the body of an animal cannot be uncompounded; I mean, it cannot consist entirely of fire, for instance, or of air. An animal, unless it has touch, can have no other sense, the animate body being always, as we have remarked, capable of tactile sensation. Now the other elements, with the exception of earth, would make sense-organs: but it is always indirectly and through media that such organs effect sensation. Touch, however, acts by direct contact with objects: hence its name. The other sense-organs, it is true, also perceive by contact, but it is by indirect contact: touch alone, it would seem, perceives directly in and through itself. Thus, then, no one of the three elements referred to can constitute the body of the animal. Nor indeed can it be of earth. For touch is a sort of mean between all tangible qualities, and its organ is receptive not only of all the distinctive qualities of earth, but also of heat and cold and all other tangible qualities. And this is why we do not perceive anything with our bones and our hair and such parts of us, namely, because they are of earth. And for the same reason plants, too, have no sensation, because they are composed of earth. Without touch, however, there can be no other sense; and the organ of this sense does not consist of earth nor of any other single element.

Thus it is evident that this is the only sense the loss of which necessarily involves the death of the animal. For it is not possible for anything that is not an animal to have this sense, nor is it necessary for anything that is an animal to have any other sense besides this. And this explains another fact. The other sensibles - I mean, colour, sound, odour - do not by their excess destroy the animal, but only the corresponding sense-organs: except incidentally, as when concurrently with the sound some thrust or blow is given, or when objects of sight or smell move something else which destroys by contact. Flavour, again, destroys only in so far as it is at the same time tactile. Tangible qualities, on the other hand, as heat, cold and hardness, if in excess, are fatal to the living animal. For excess of any sensible object is fatal to the organ, and so consequently excess of the tangible object is fatal to touch. And it is by this sense that the life of the animal is defined, touch having been proved to be indispensable to the existence of an animal. Hence excess in tangible qualities destroys not only the sense-organ, but also the animal itself. For touch is the one sense that the animal cannot do without. The other senses which it possesses are, as we have said, the means, not to its being, but to well-being. Thus the animal has sight to see with, because it lives in air or water or, speaking generally, in a transparent medium. It has taste on account of what is pleasant and painful, to the end that it may perceive what is pleasant in food and feel desire and be impelled to movement. It has hearing in order that information may be conveyed to it, and a tongue, that in its turn it may convey information to its fellow.

AZILOTH ||| BOOKS

Aziloth Books publishes a wide range of titles ranging from hard-to-find esoteric books - *Parehment Books* - to classic works on fiction, politics and philosophy - *Cathedral Classics*. Our newest venture is *Aziloth Books Children's Classics*, with vibrant new covers and illustrations to complement some of the world's very best children's tales. All our imprints are offered to the reader at a competitive price and through as many mediums and outlets as possible.

We are committed to excellent book production and strive, whenever possible, to add value to our titles with original images, maps and author introductions. With the premium on space in most modern dwellings, we also endeavour - within the limits of good book design - to make our products as slender as possible, allowing more books to be fitted into a given bookshelf area.

We are a small, approachable company and would love to hear any of your comments and suggestions on our plans, products, or indeed on absolutely anything.

Aziloth Books is also interested in hearing from aspiring authors whom we might publish. We look forward to meeting you.

Contact us (Drs. K. & L. Laidler) at: info@azilothbooks.com

Aziloth Books, Rimey Law, Rookhope, Co. Durham
DL13 2BL
t: 01388-517600 e: info@azilothbooks.com w: www.azilothbooks.com

Parchment Books enshrines the concept of the oneness of all true religious traditions - that "the light shines from many different lanterns". Our list below offers titles from both eastern and western spiritual traditions, including Christian, Judaic, Islamic, Daoist, Hindu and Buddhist mystical texts, as well as books on alchemy, hermeticism, paganism, etc..

By bringing together such spiritual texts, we hope to make esoteric and occult knowledge more readily available to those ready to receive it. We do not publish grimoires or any titles pertaining to the left hand path. Titles include:

Abandonment to Divine Providence	Jean-Pierre de Caussade
Corpus Hermeticum	G. R. S. Mead (trans.)
The Holy Rule of St Benedict	St. Benedict of Nursia
The Way of Perfection	St. Teresa of Avila
The Cloud Upon the Sanctuary	Karl von Eckhartshausen
The Confession of St Patrick	St. Patrick
The Outline of Sanity	G. K. Chesterton
The Dialogue Of St Catherine Of Siena	St. Catherine of Siena
Esoteric Christianity	Annie Besant
The Spiritual Exercises of St. Ignatius	St. Ignatius of Loyola
Dark Night of the Soul	St. John of the Cross
The Gospel of Thomas	Anonymous
St. Francis	G. K. Chesterton
The Imitation of Christ	Thomas à Kempis
The Interior Castle	St. Teresa of Avila
Songs of Innocence & Experience	William Blake
The Marriage of Heaven & Hell	William Blake
The Secret of the Rosary	St. Louis Marie de Montfort
From Ritual to Romance	Jessie L. Weston
The God of the Witches	Margaret Murray

Obtainable at all good online and local bookstores.
View Aziloth Books' full list at: www.azilothbooks.com

Cathedral Classics

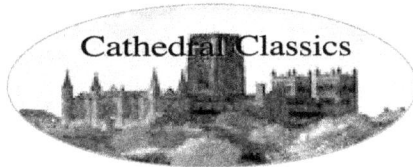

Cathedral Classics hosts an array of classic literature, from erudite ancient tomes to avant-garde, twentieth-century masterpieces, all of which deserve a place in your home. All the world's great novelists are here, Jane Austen, Dickens, Conrad, Arthur Machen and Henry James, brushing shoulders with such disparate luminaries as Sun Tzu, Mareus Aurelius, Kipling, Friedrich Nietzsche, Machiavelli, and Omar Khayam. A small selection is detailed below:

Frankenstein	Mary Shelley
The Time Machine; The Invisible Man	H. G. Wells
The Prince	Niccolo Machiavelli
The Rubaiyat of Omar Khayyam	Omar Khayyam
Heart of Darkness; The Secret Agent	Joseph Conrad
Persuasion; Northanger Abbey	Jane Austen
The Picture of Dorian Gray	Oscar Wilde
Candide	Voltaire
The Coming Race	Bulwer Lytton
The Adventures of Sherlock Holmes	Arthur Conan Doyle
The Thirty-Nine Steps	John Buchan
Beyond Good and Evil	Friedrich Nietzsche
Washington Square	Henry James
The Red Badge of Courage	Stephen Crane
Self-Reliance, & Other Essays (series 1&2)	Ralph W. Emmerson
The Art of War	Sun Tzu
A Christmas Carol	Charles Dickens
The Gambler; The Double	Fyodor Dostoyevsky
To the Lighthouse; Mrs Dalloway	Virginia Wolf
The Sorrows of Young Werther	Johann W. Goethe
Leaves of Grass - 1855 edition	Walt Whitman
Analects	Confucius
Beowulf	Anonymous
Agnes Grey	Anne Bronte
Utopia	Thomas More

Obtainable at all good online and local bookstores.
View Aziloth Books' full list at: www.azilothbooks.com

AZILOTH BOOKS | CHILDREN'S Classics

Aziloth Books is passionate about bringing the very best in children's classics fiction to the next generation of book-lovers. Renowned for its original design and outstanding quality, our highly successful list has something to suit every age and interest. Titles include:

The Railway Children	Edith Nesbit
5 Children and It	Edith Nesbit
Anne of Green Gables	Lucy Maud Montgomery
What Katy Did	Susan Coolidge
What Katy Did Next	Susan Coolidge
Puck of Pook's Hill	Rudyard Kipling
The Jungle Books	Rudyard Kipling
Just So Stories	Rudyard Kipling
Alice Through the Looking Glass	Charles Dodgson
Alice's Adventures in Wonderland	Charles Dodgson
Black Beauty	Anna Sewell
The War of the Worlds	H. G. Wells
The Time Machine	H. G .Wells
The Sleeper Awakes	H. G. Wells
The Invisible Man	H. G. Wells
Treasure Island	Robert Louis Stevenson
Dr Jekyll and Mr Hyde	Robert Louis Stevenson
Kidnapped	Robert Louis Stevenson
Catriona (David Balfour)	Robert Louis Stevenson
The Water Babies	Charles Kingsley
The First Men in the Moon	Jules Verne
The Lost World	Sir Arthur Conan Doyle
A Christmas Carol	Charles Dickens
Call of the Wild	Jack London
Greenmantle	John Buchan
The Secret Garden	Frances Hodgson Burnett
A Little Princess	Frances Hodgson Burnett
Peter Pan	J. M. Barrie

Obtainable at all good online and local bookstores.
View Aziloth Books' full list at: www.azilothbooks.com